Bringing Origami to Life

Other books by John Montroll:

Origami Sculptures

Prehistoric Origami *Dinosaurs and Other Creatures*

Origami Sea Life by John Montroll and Robert J. Lang

African Animals in Origami

Origami Inside-Out

North American Animals in Origami

Mythological Creatures and the Chinese Zodiac in Origami

Teach Yourself Origami

Animal Origami for the Enthusiast

Origami for the Enthusiast

Easy Origami

Birds in Origami

Favorite Animals in Origami

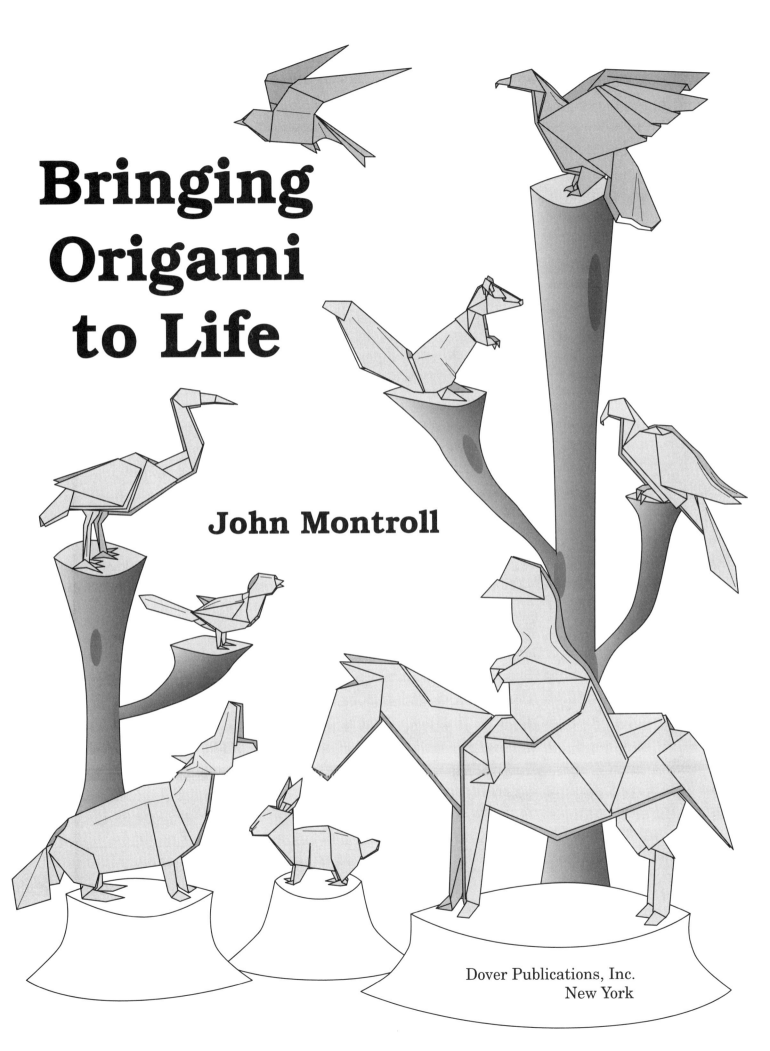

Bringing Origami to Life

John Montroll

Dover Publications, Inc.
New York

To Andy, Barbara Anne, and Sarah

Published in Canada by General Publishing Company, Ltd., 30 Lesmill Road, Don Mills, Toronto, Ontario.
Published in the United Kingdom by Constable and Company, Ltd., 3 The Lanchesters, 162–164 Fulham Palace Road, London W6 9ER.

Bibliographical Note

This work is first published in 1999 in separate editions by Antroll Publishing Company, Maryland, and Dover Publications, Inc., New York.

Library of Congress Cataloging-in-Publication Data

Montroll, John.
    Bringing origami to life / John Montroll.
        p.   cm.
    ISBN 0-486-40714-4 (pbk.)
    1. Origami.   I. Title.
TT870.M553   1999
736'.982—dc21
                                        99-41234
                                        CIP

Manufactured in the United States of America
Dover Publications, Inc., 31 East 2nd Street, Mineola, N.Y. 11501

Introduction

Come learn how to fold a hungry hippo, sitting cat, howling coyote, and many more exciting origami animals. These projects represent many innovative styles of folding that emphasize detail while requiring fewer steps. Extra detail is given to some of the more complex models, such as the ibis, crocodile, and horse with rider.

Each model has a story to tell. Following the diagrams is similar to reading a mystery. Before you start, you know what the model should look like, yet do not know what it takes to fold it. Through the folding process, you are solving a mystery, possibly wondering how the first folds can be used, and later seeing how it all fits together.

Though all the models shown here can be done from standard origami paper, a higher quality can be achieved by wet-folding. This technique is growing in popularity amongst folders, and a lesson in its use is provided; wet-folding allows the models to be more easily molded and shaped, and ultimately more permanent. Actual photographs show its use.

There is an emphasis on structures and bases throughout this book; several of the models are related to each other through variations. For example, the eagle and parrot use similar techniques for the head, legs, and wings, but the parrot's tail is longer. The bear and horse use similar structures, while more paper is given to the horse's neck.

I have included only models which can be folded from one uncut square. An inexperienced folder should work from the beginning to the end of the book. The difficulty level increases as you progress, and some of the models use techniques from the previous ones.

The illustrations conform to the internationally accepted Randlett-Yoshizawa conventions. The colored side of origami paper is represented by the shadings in the diagrams. Origami paper can be found in many hobby shops or purchased by mail from OrigamiUSA, 15 West 77th Street, New York, NY 10024-5192 or from Dover Publications, Inc., 31 East 2nd Street, Mineola, NY 11501. Large sheets are easier to use than small ones.

Many people helped make this book possible. I want to thank Michael LaFosse for his help with the wet folding technique. I also wish to thank John Carlos Marino, a student at St. Anselm's Abbey School, for the photographs. Thanks to my editors, Jan Polish and Charley Montroll. Of course I also thank the many folders who proof-read the diagrams.

John Montroll

Contents

★   Simple
★★   Intermediate
★★★   Complex

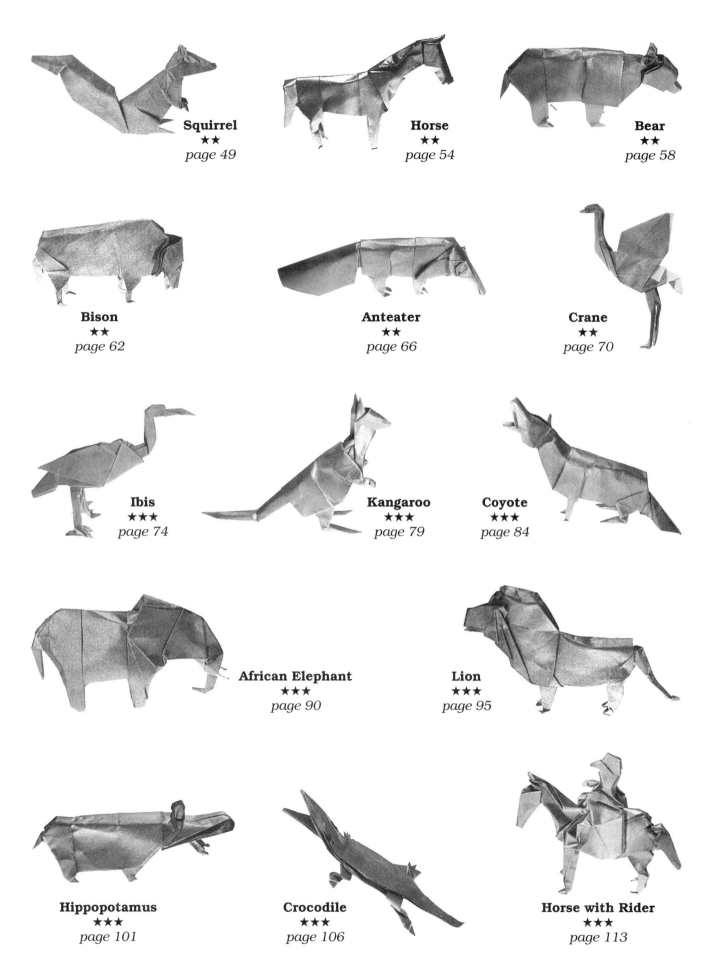

Squirrel
★★
page 49

Horse
★★
page 54

Bear
★★
page 58

Bison
★★
page 62

Anteater
★★
page 66

Crane
★★
page 70

Ibis
★★★
page 74

Kangaroo
★★★
page 79

Coyote
★★★
page 84

African Elephant
★★★
page 90

Lion
★★★
page 95

Hippopotamus
★★★
page 101

Crocodile
★★★
page 106

Horse with Rider
★★★
page 113

Symbols

Lines

— — — — — — — —   Valley fold, fold in front.

— · — · — · — · —   Mountain fold, fold behind.

—————————   Crease line.

· · · · · · · · · · · · · · ·   X-ray or guide line.

Arrows

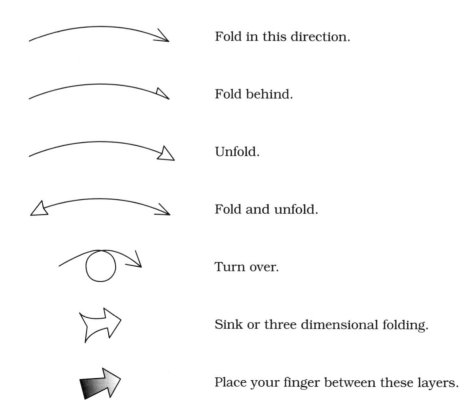

Fold in this direction.

Fold behind.

Unfold.

Fold and unfold.

Turn over.

Sink or three dimensional folding.

Place your finger between these layers.

Wet-Folding

Much of the most inspiring examples of today's origami sculptures are produced using the wet-folding technique. Pioneered and promoted by Japanese origami master Akira Yoshizawa, this method of paperfolding allows for a great range of expression and form. Soft, curving forms become possible and subtle shaping will bring your models to life.

Choosing paper to wet-fold is largely a matter of experimentation with the types of papers that are available to you and what you can afford. Generally, the heavier, stiffly sized art papers are a good type to start with; there are many brands on the market and they come in a wide range of colors and textures. A basic rule to follow is the greater the complexity of the model, the thinner the paper you should use. Simple models can make use of very heavy papers. Always work with larger size papers to start: 12" to 18" square is a good range for most of the models in this book.

A common mistake that beginners make is wetting the paper too much. Actually, the paper should look dry. Only enough water is added so that the paper becomes pliant, like a piece of leather. Paper that is too wet will easily be damaged during folding. It is important to wet both sides of the paper in order to prevent curling of the sheet.

There are several ways to wet your paper. One is the wet sponge method: wipe a damp sponge lightly over the entire surface of both sides of the paper. Do not rub too hard or you will abrade the paper's finish and end up with a fuzzy model. Another way to wet the paper is with a mist of water from a plant mister. Hold the paper in the air and lightly, but evenly, spray both sides of the paper. Have a small, damp, cloth towel to smooth the beads of moisture evenly over the paper's surface. Which ever method you use you should allow time for the paper to absorb the water. As you work your paper will begin to dry out and you will re-wet the paper in any areas that become stiff and difficult to shape. In any case, work gently and patiently; you should not put sharp creases in with your fingernails. Explore expressive forms as you fold and give some life and personality to your work.

As you approach the finishing stages of your folding you may find that your model is too damp to leave on its own. Using strips of paper toweling or soft twine, you can secure the form of the model and let it dry overnight. Any areas that you are not satisfied with can be re-wet and shaped separately.

An alternate to wetting the entire sheet is to only wet the paper along the lines that are to be folded. This method is most useful on papers that expand greatly. An example of this type of wet-folding is given in the traditional crane project in the book. Follow the instructions on when and where to dampen the paper to get a feel for this method.

We hope that this introduction to wet-folding will contribute greatly to your enjoyment of the art, and that you will receive satisfaction from producing beautiful, long-lasting models that will be an inspiration and source of enjoyment for many years to come.

Crane

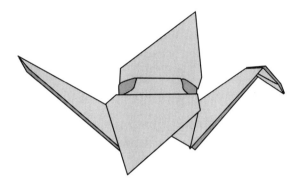

This model is used as a lesson in wet-folding. I hope you already know how to fold the crane. If not, it is important to know. This traditional bird is a symbol of hope and peace.

Begin with a bowl of water, sponge, napkins, hard surface to fold on, and thick paper as described on the previous page. I have made up a symbol, shown as a thick grey line, to represent the sponge strokes. **Only lightly dampen the paper with each stroke; do not make it dripping wet.** Note that for the first several steps you are only dampening where the folds will be made.

1
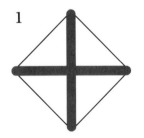

Dampen the diagonals with a sponge and turn over.

2

Dampen the diagonals on this side.

3
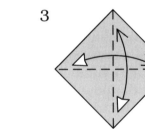

Fold and unfold. Fold gently. Instead of using your fingernail or sliding your finger along the folded edge, use all your fingers over the creased line and pat the paper from the center to each end along the folded edge.

4
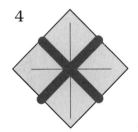

Dampen on both sides.

5

6
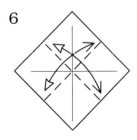

Fold and unfold.

7

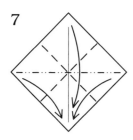

Collapse along
the creases.

8

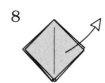

This is the preliminary
fold. Unfold to dampen.

9

This is the key step for almost
all wet-folded models. Now that
a few creases are there, dampen
the whole paper on both sides.
They can be done in large or
small strokes.

10

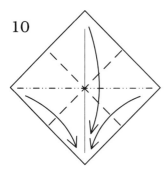

Refold.

11

Dampen as many layers
as possible on all sides. It
is ok to open the paper.

12

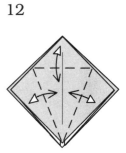

Fold and unfold.
Repeat the kite
folds behind.

13

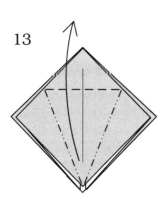

Petal-fold. Repeat behind.

14

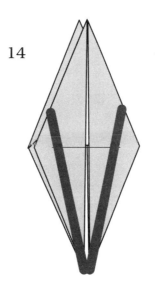

Dampen as many layers
as possible on all sides.

15

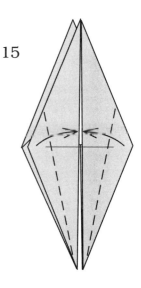

Repeat behind.

16

Dampen as many layers as possible. Repeat behind.

17

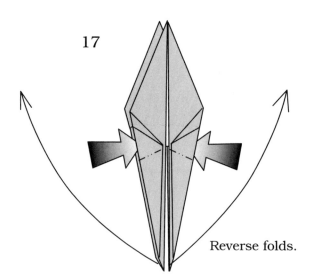

Reverse folds.

18

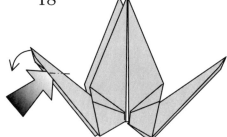

Reverse-fold.

19

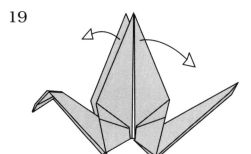

Pull the wings apart and let the body open.

20

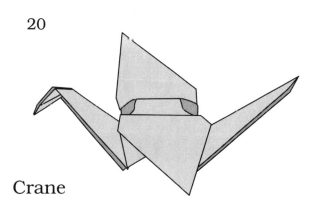

Crane

Duck

For the first model, the duck is a simple example with three dimensional folding. Towards the end, the beak, neck, body, and tail become round. While shaping the duck in these last steps, make soft creases. The next few models build upon the folding method used for this duck. Though it does not need to be wet-folded, you can see how wet-folding enhances its shape. Note that the diagrams no longer specify the dampening locations. See the diagrams for the traditional crane for help.

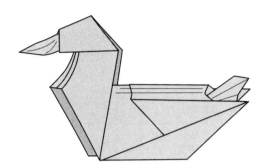

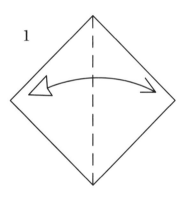

1

Fold and unfold.

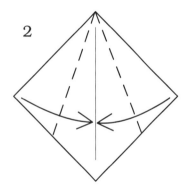

2

Kite-fold.

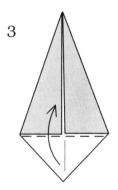

3

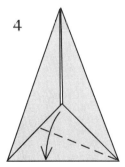

4

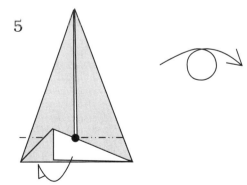

5

Fold behind at the dot and turn over.

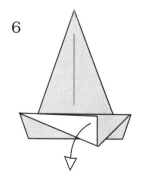

6

Unfold.

7

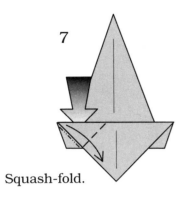

Squash-fold.

8

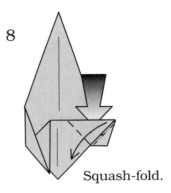

Squash-fold.

9

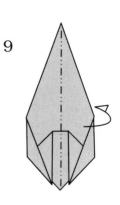

10

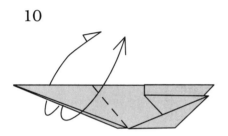

Outside-reverse-fold.

11

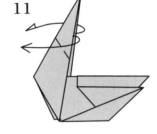

Outside-reverse-fold.

12

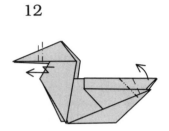

Crimp-fold the beak and tail.

13

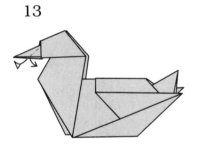

Open and flatten the beak. The duck will now become three-dimensional.

14

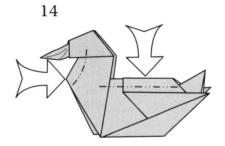

Push in the neck and back, rounding them.

15

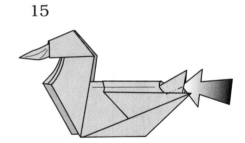

Spread the tail.

16

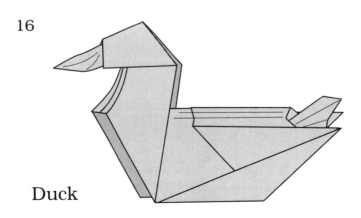

Duck

Swan

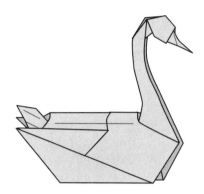

The method for folding the swan is similar to the duck, but the swan has a longer neck.

1

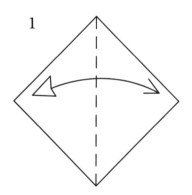

Fold and unfold.

2

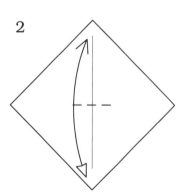

Fold up and unfold, creasing only in the center.

3

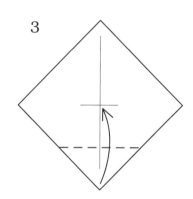

4

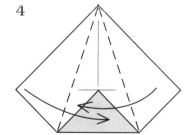

5

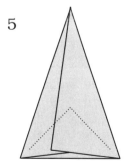

Bring the hidden triangle to the front.

6

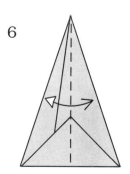

Fold and unfold.

7

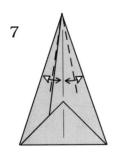

Fold and unfold.

8

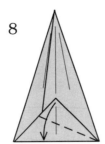

9

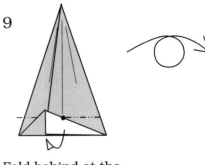

Fold behind at the dot and turn over.

10

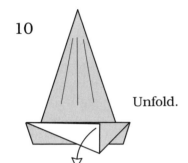

Unfold.

11

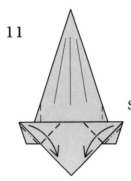

Squash folds.

12

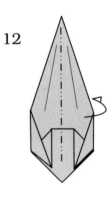

13

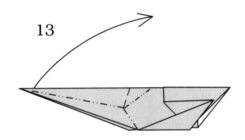

Double-rabbit-ear.

14

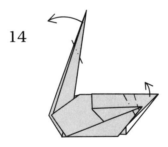

Reverse-fold the neck and crimp-fold the tail.

15

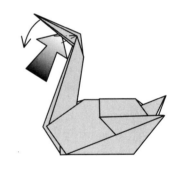

Open the head while folding it down.

16

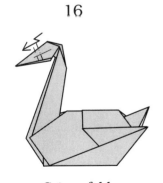

Crimp-fold.

17

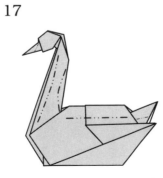

Curve the beak, neck, body, and tail.

18

Swan

Goose

For this goose, feet are added to the duck design. Compare step 20 of the goose with step 9 of the duck to see the similarities in structure.

1

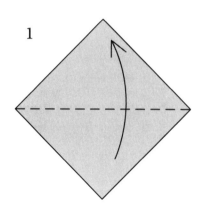

2

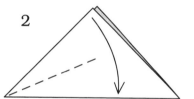

Fold down, creasing only the left side.

3

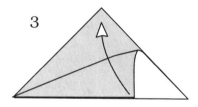

Unfold.

4

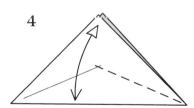

Fold and unfold.

5

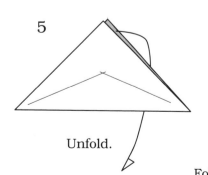

Unfold.

6

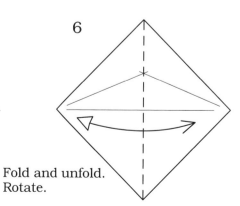

Fold and unfold.
Rotate.

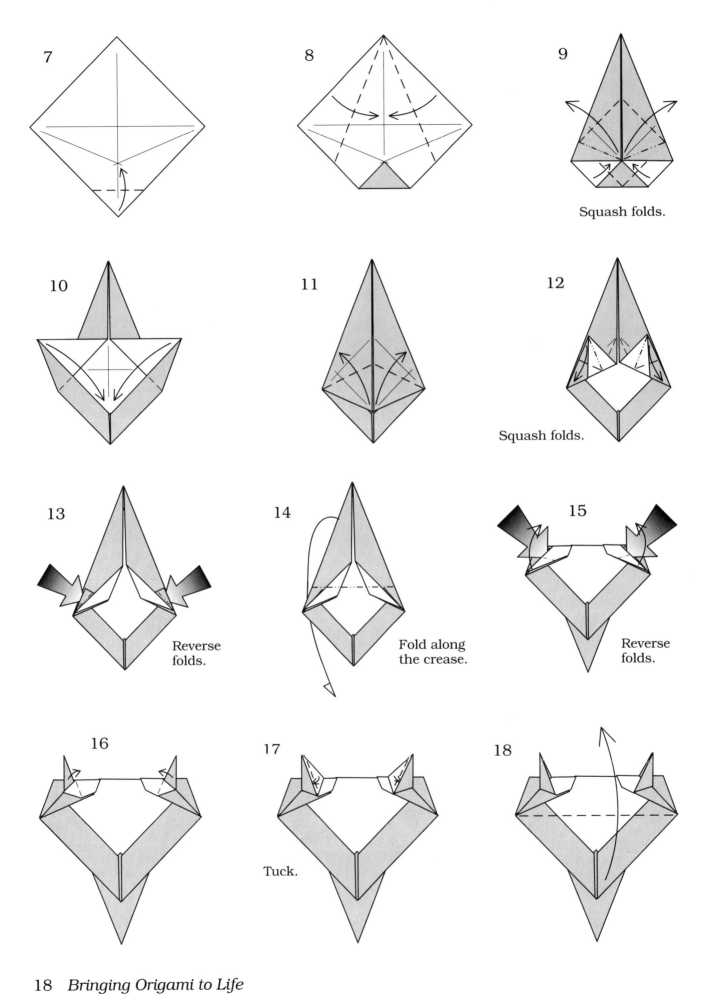

7

8

9

Squash folds.

10

11

12

Squash folds.

13

Reverse
folds.

14

Fold along
the crease.

15

Reverse
folds.

16

17

Tuck.

18

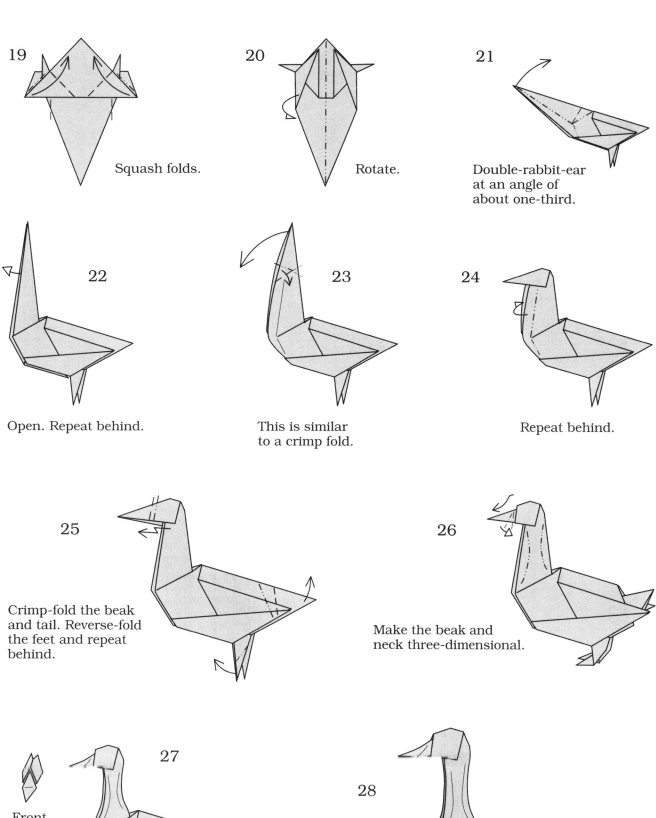

19   Squash folds.

20   Rotate.

21   Double-rabbit-ear at an angle of about one-third.

22   Open. Repeat behind.

23   This is similar to a crimp fold.

24   Repeat behind.

25   Crimp-fold the beak and tail. Reverse-fold the feet and repeat behind.

26   Make the beak and neck three-dimensional.

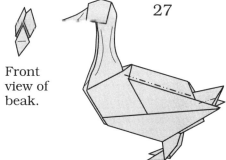

Front view of beak.

27   Make the body and tail three-dimensional.

28

Goose

Sparrow

The structure used for the duck, swan, and goose has been further developed to form a longer tail. Compare step 18 of the sparrow with step 20 of the goose.

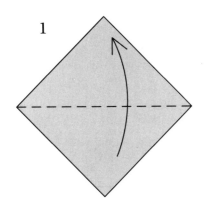

1

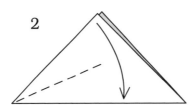

2

Fold down, creasing only the left side.

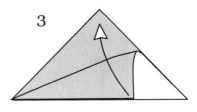

3

Unfold.

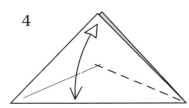

4

Fold and unfold.

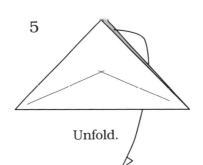

5

Unfold.

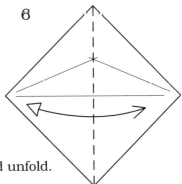

6

Fold and unfold.
Rotate.

7

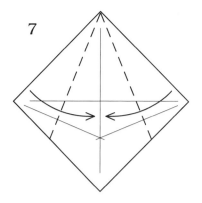

8

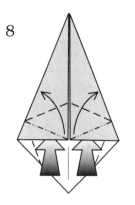

Squash folds.

9

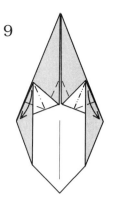

Squash folds.

10

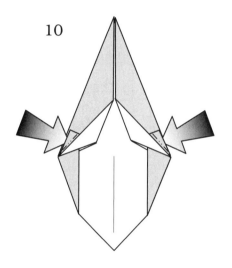

Reverse folds.

11

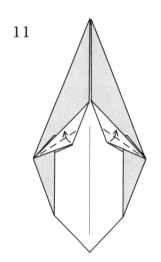

Spread squash folds.

12

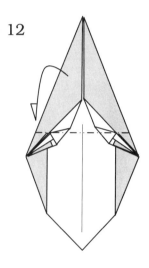

13

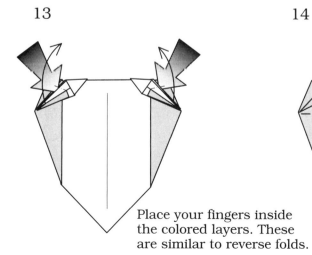

Place your fingers inside
the colored layers. These
are similar to reverse folds.

14

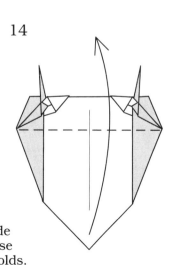

15

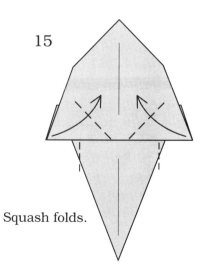

Squash folds.

Sparrow 21

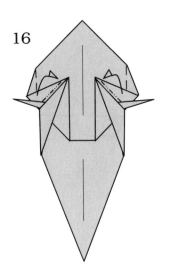

16

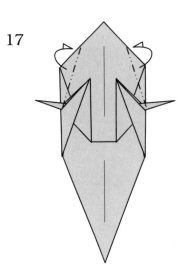

17

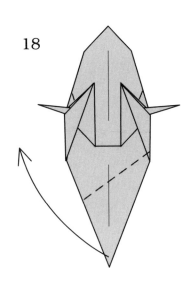

18

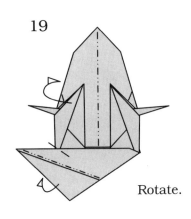

19

Rotate.

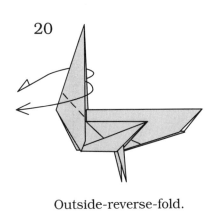

20

Outside-reverse-fold.

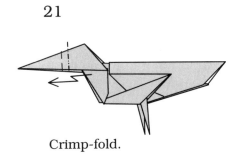

21

Crimp-fold.

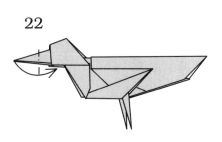

22

Reverse-fold.

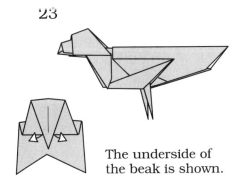

23

The underside of
the beak is shown.

24

The underside
of the beak.

25

26

27

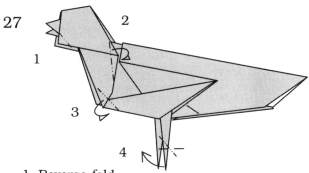

1. Reverse-fold.
4. Crimp-fold.
Repeat behind.

28

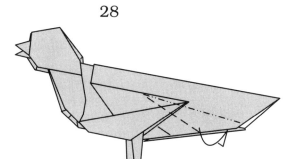

All these folds are now
three-dimensional.

29

The sparrow is now three-dimensional.
Round the top of the head and back.

30

Sparrow

Swallow

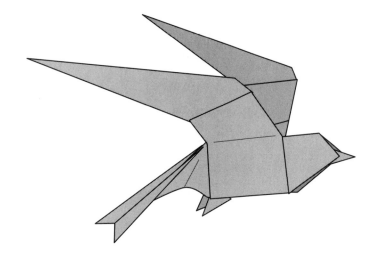

The swallow uses a different structure than the previous birds. The emphasis in the design is to capture the long wings and split tail.

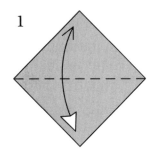

1

Fold and unfold.

2

Fold and unfold.

3

Rabbit-ear.

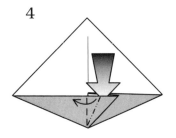

4

Squash-fold.

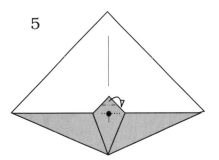

5

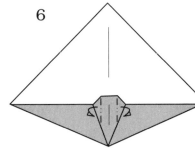

6

Rotate.

7

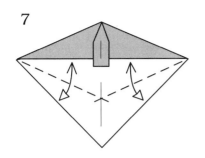

Fold and unfold.

8

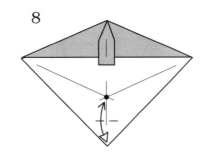

Fold and unfold.

9

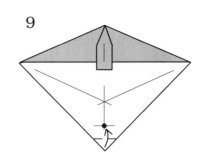

10

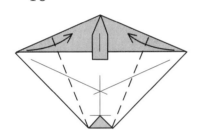

11

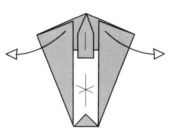

Unfold.

12

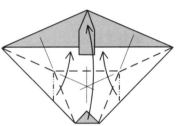

13

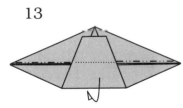

14

15

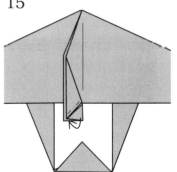

Reverse-fold.

16

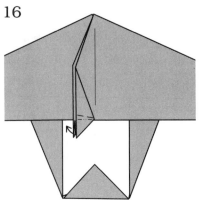

Repeat behind.

17

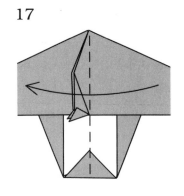

18

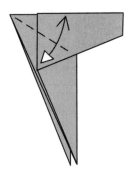

Fold and unfold.
Repeat behind.

19

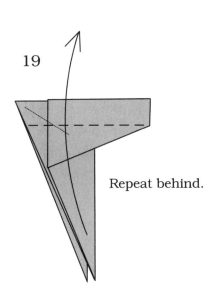

Repeat behind.

20

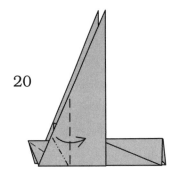

Squash-fold.
Repeat behind.

21

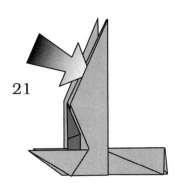

Bring the paper over
the darker layer.
Repeat behind.

22

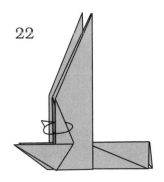

Fold inside.
Repeat behind.

23

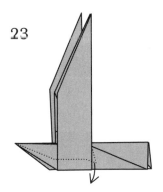

Slide down the feet.

24

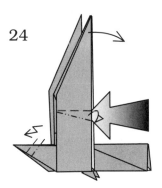

Crimp-fold the beak and
wings. Repeat behind.

25

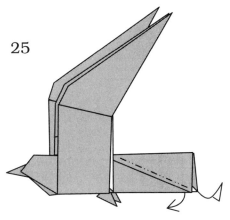

Spread the tail.

26

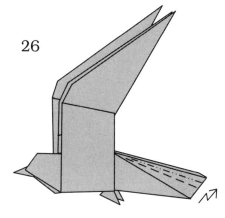

The tail is three-dimensional. The valley fold line is at the center, and the mountain fold is half way between.

27

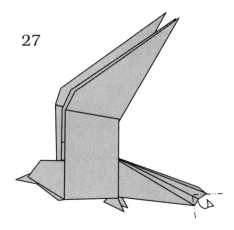

28

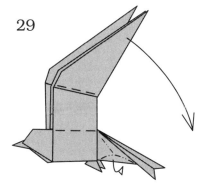

Repeat behind.

29

Repeat behind.

30

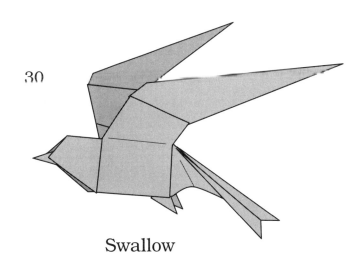

Swallow

Cat

For the first mammal in this series, I present a cat. The large number of steps does not indicate high difficulty, since many steps just unfold prior folds. Often when I design I develop new intermediate folding structures, or bases. Sometimes they are only used in one model, although in this case the base (step 25) is used again for the dog. This cat has a seamless closed back, considered to be the most artistic and realistic representation. The rest of the mammals in this collection also have seamless closed backs.

1

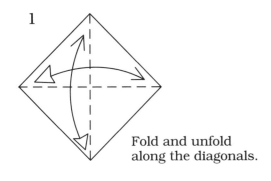

Fold and unfold along the diagonals.

2

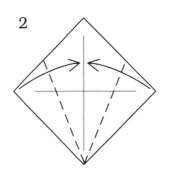

3

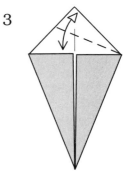

Fold and unfold.

4

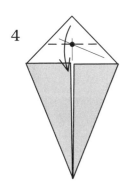

5

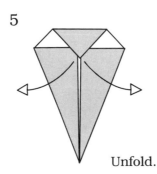

Unfold.

6

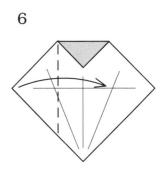

7

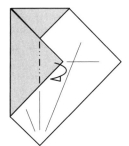

8

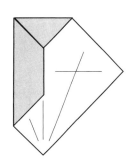

Repeat steps 6–7
on the right.

9

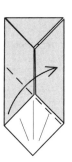

10

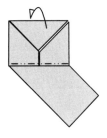

11

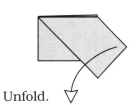

Unfold.

12

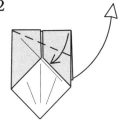

13

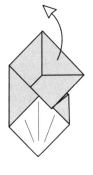

Unfold.

14

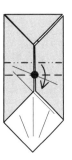

15

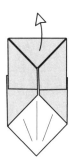

Unfold.

16

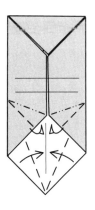

17

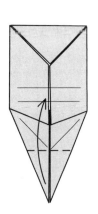

18

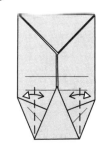

Fold and unfold.

Cat 29

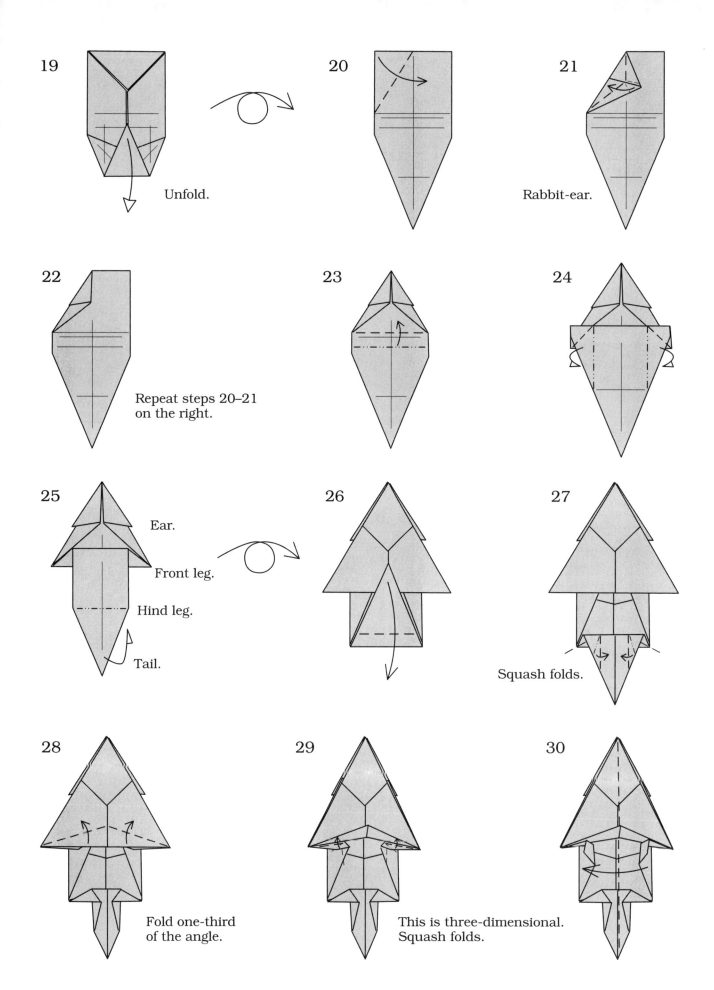

19

Unfold.

20

21

Rabbit-ear.

22

Repeat steps 20–21
on the right.

23

24

25

Ear.

Front leg.

Hind leg.

Tail.

26

27

Squash folds.

28

Fold one-third
of the angle.

29

This is three-dimensional.
Squash folds.

30

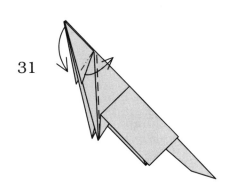

31

Squash-fold.

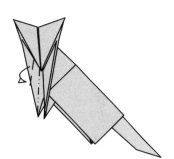

32

The head is not flat.

33

Bring the darker paper above. Repeat behind.

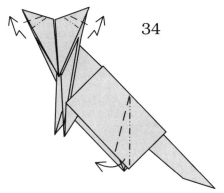

34

Crimp-fold the ears and legs.

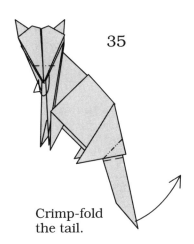

35

Crimp-fold the tail.

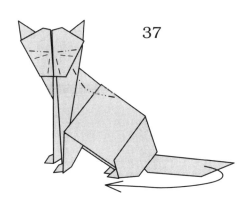

36

Repeat behind.

37

Shape the head, body, and tail.

38

Sitting Cat

Dog

The dog uses the same base as the cat. A hidden corner is pulled out to form the mouth.

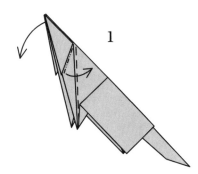

1

Begin with step 31 of the cat. Crimp-fold.

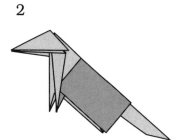

2

Bring the darker paper to the front. Repeat behind.

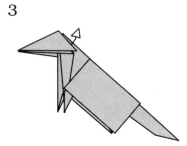

3

Pull out. Repeat behind.

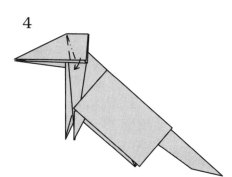

4

Repeat behind.

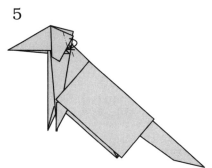

5

Reverse-fold. Repeat behind.

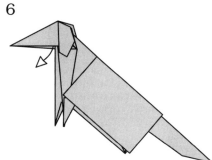

6

Pull out the lower jaw.

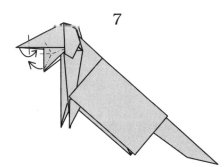

7

Double-rabbit-ear the lower jaw. Reverse-fold the nose.

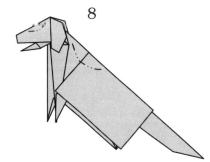

8

Continue with step 34 of the cat for the legs and tail.

9

Sitting Dog

Eagle

This eagle has a great deal of detail, even though it only takes 22 steps to fold. I have tried to design the animals here as efficiently as possible without sacrificing detail. The head comes from the center of the square, the wings from opposite corners and the feet and tail from the remaining corners, as you can see from the base (step 10).

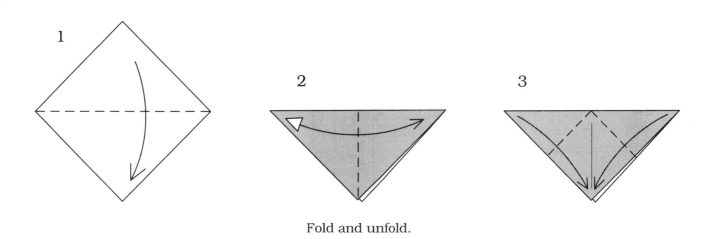

Fold and unfold.

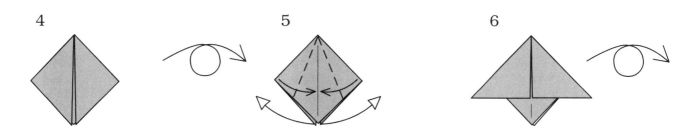

7

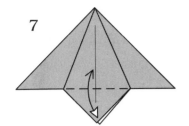

Fold one layer
up and unfold.

8

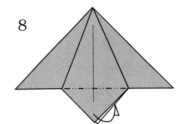

9

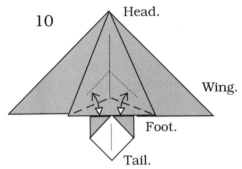

10

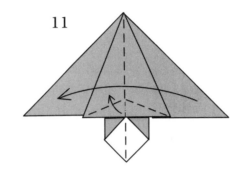

Head.

Wing.

Foot.

Tail.

Fold and unfold.

11

Reverse-fold.
Repeat behind.

12

13

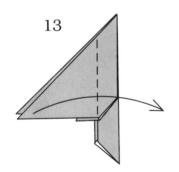

Repeat behind.

14

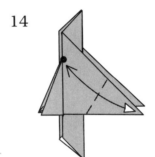

Fold and unfold.
Repeat behind.

15

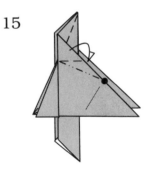

Fold inside.
Repeat behind.

16

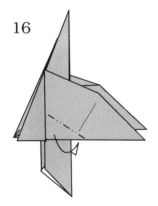

Fold inside.
Repeat behind.

17

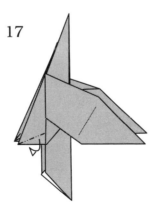

Fold inside.
Repeat behind.

18

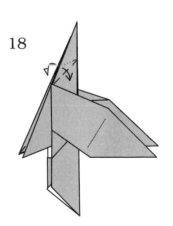

Crimp-fold.

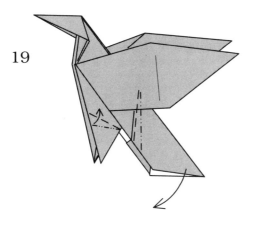

19

Repeat behind for the legs.
Crimp-fold the tail.

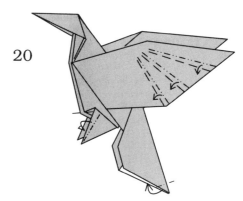

20

Repeat behind.

21

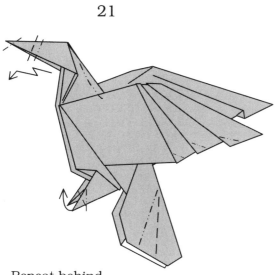

Repeat behind.

22

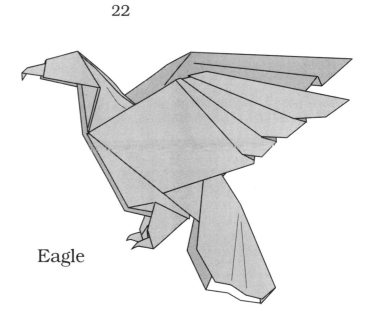

Eagle

Parrot

The parrot uses a structure similar to the eagle but with a longer tail. To make this happen, the head comes from an off-center point on the square. Compare the base for the parrot, step 22, with step 10 of the eagle.

1

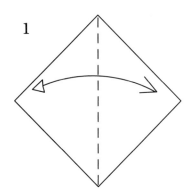

Fold and unfold.

2

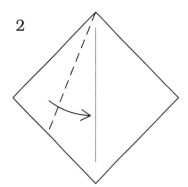

Crease lightly.

3

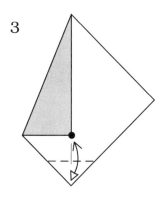

Fold and unfold.

4

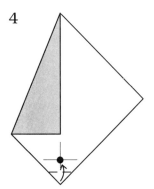

5

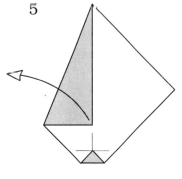

Unfold.

6

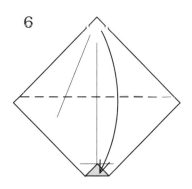

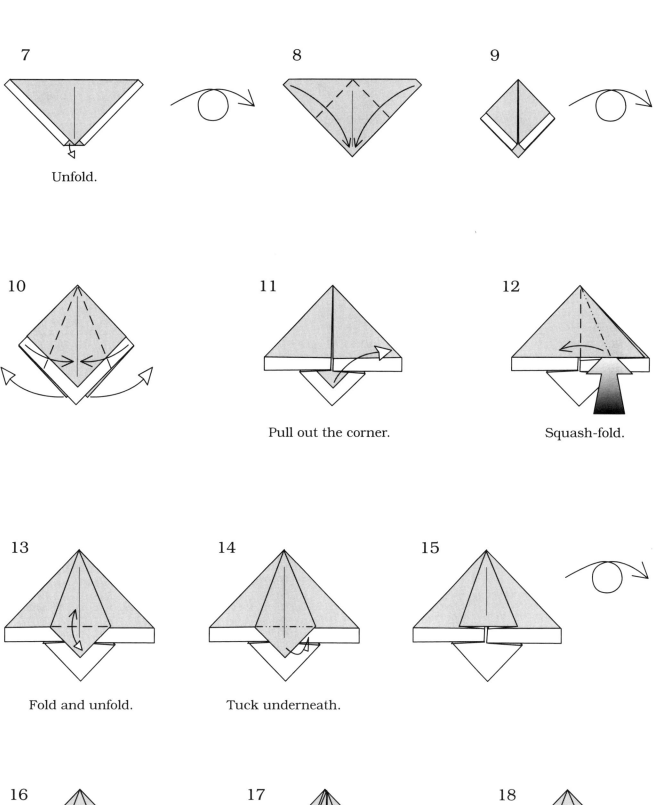

7

Unfold.

8

9

10

11

Pull out the corner.

12

Squash-fold.

13

Fold and unfold.

14

Tuck underneath.

15

16

Petal-fold.

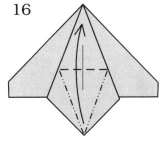

17

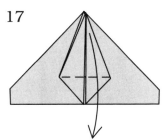

18

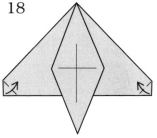

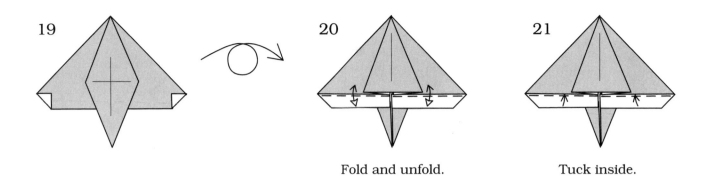

19　　20 Fold and unfold.　　21 Tuck inside.

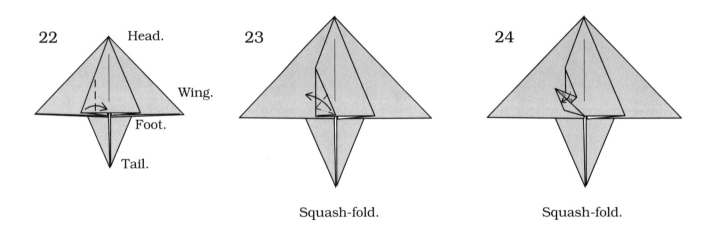

22 Head. Wing. Foot. Tail.　　23 Squash-fold.　　24 Squash-fold.

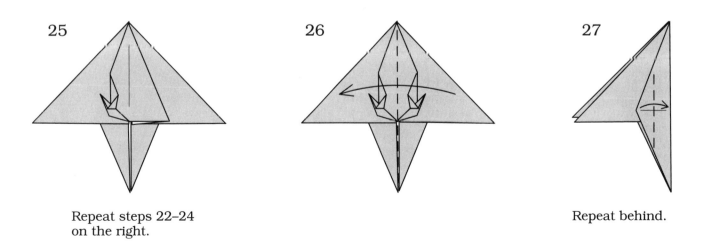

25 Repeat steps 22–24 on the right.　　26　　27 Repeat behind.

28

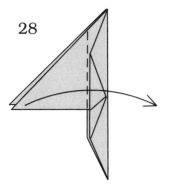

Repeat behind.

29

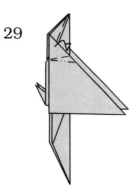

Repeat behind.

30

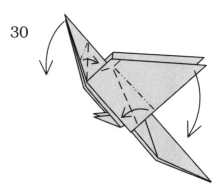

1. Crimp-fold the head.
2. Reverse-fold the feet.
3. Fold the wing down.
Repeat behind.

31

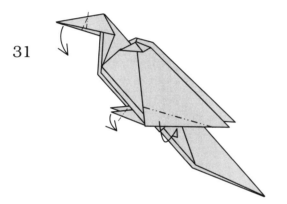

1. Crimp-fold the head.
2. Reverse-fold the feet.
3. Reverse-fold the wing.
Repeat behind.

32

Repeat behind.

33

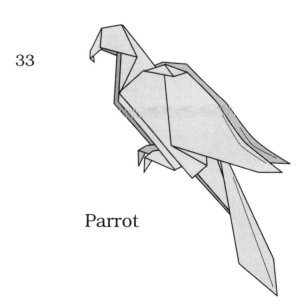

Parrot

Apatosaurus

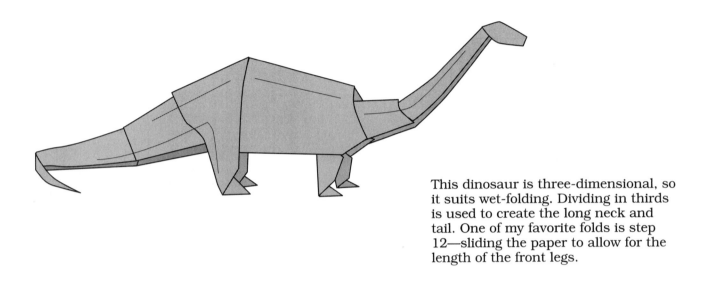

This dinosaur is three-dimensional, so it suits wet-folding. Dividing in thirds is used to create the long neck and tail. One of my favorite folds is step 12—sliding the paper to allow for the length of the front legs.

1

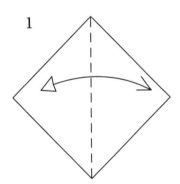

Fold and unfold.

2

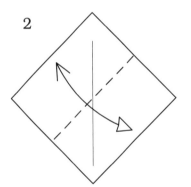

Fold and unfold.

3

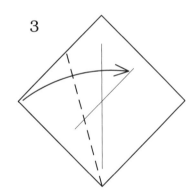

Fold the corner to the line.

4

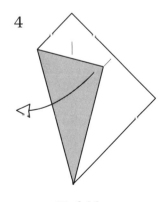

Unfold.

5

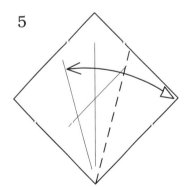

Fold to the crease and unfold.

6

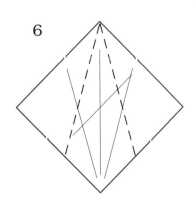

Repeat steps 3–5 on the top.

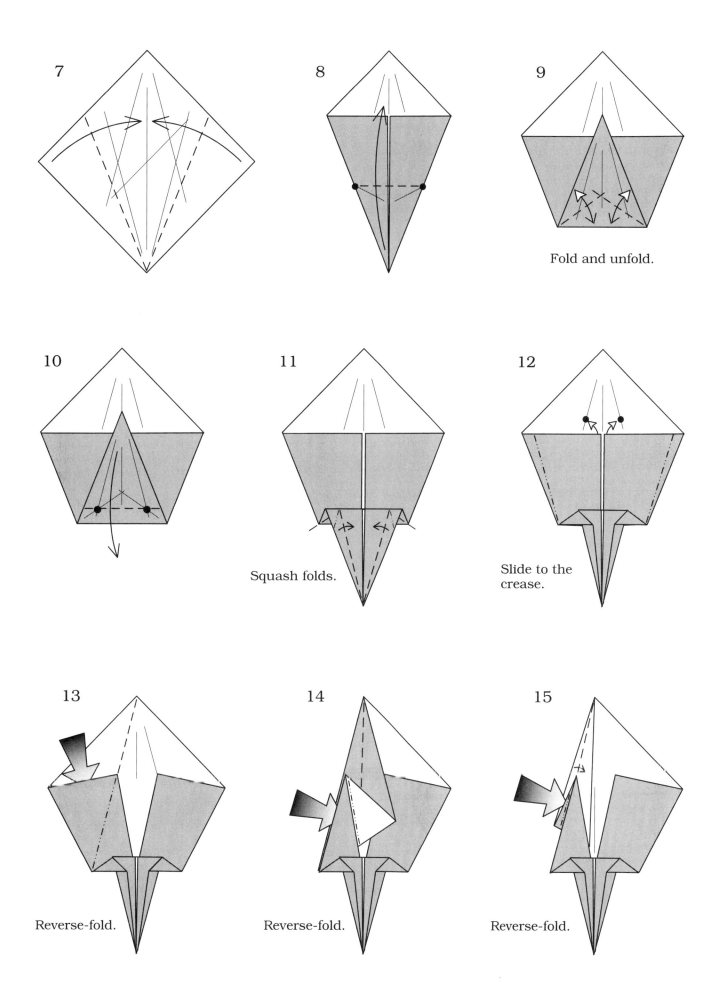

7

8

9

Fold and unfold.

10

11

Squash folds.

12

Slide to the crease.

13

Reverse-fold.

14

Reverse-fold.

15

Reverse-fold.

16

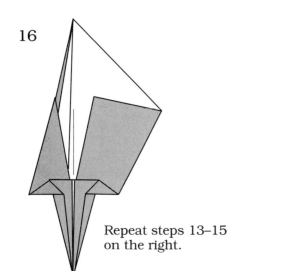

Repeat steps 13–15 on the right.

17

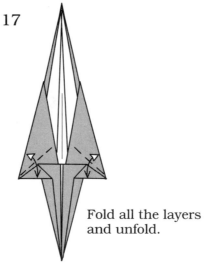

Fold all the layers and unfold.

18

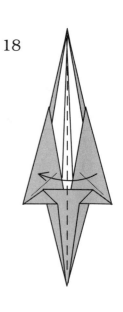

19

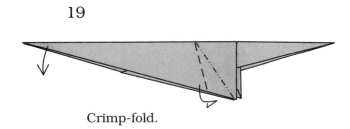

Crimp-fold.

20

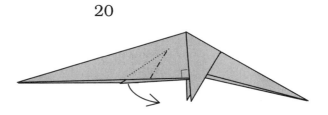

Note the right angle by the hind legs. Reverse-fold. Repeat behind.

21

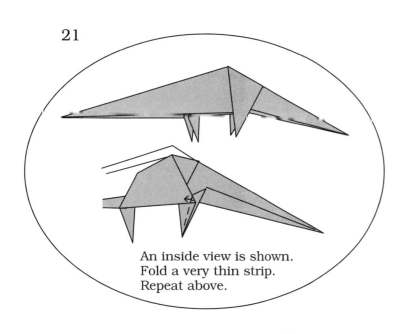

An inside view is shown. Fold a very thin strip. Repeat above.

22

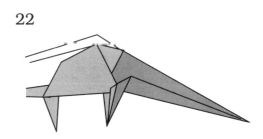

Bring the darker paper to the front. Repeat above.

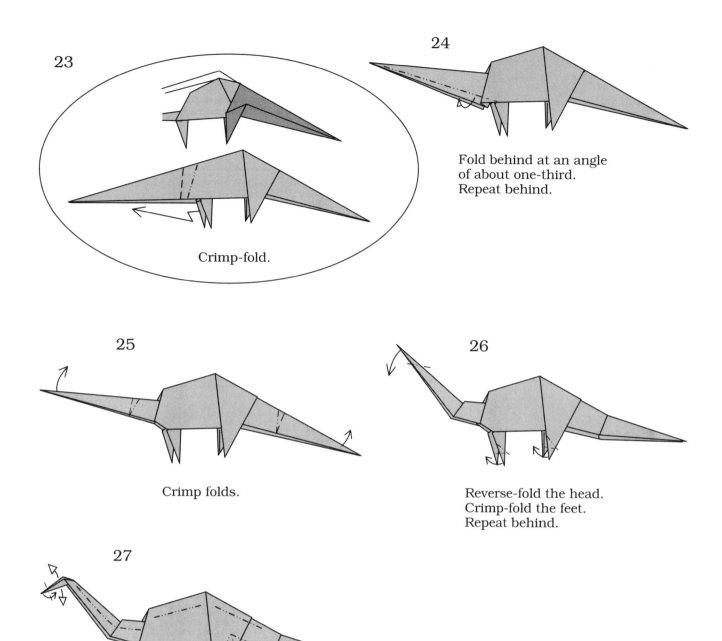

23

Crimp-fold.

24

Fold behind at an angle
of about one-third.
Repeat behind.

25

Crimp folds.

26

Reverse-fold the head.
Crimp-fold the feet.
Repeat behind.

27

Open and shape the head, back, and tail.

28

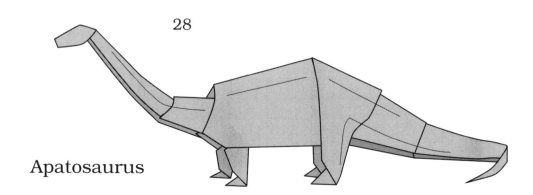

Apatosaurus

Rabbit

For this rabbit an interesting base, step 31, was developed to allow for long ears with the seamless closed back. The corners are used for the head, front legs, and tail.

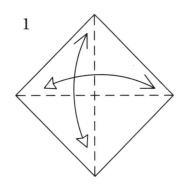

Fold and unfold.

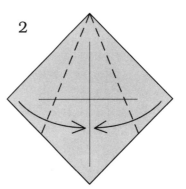

Kite-fold.

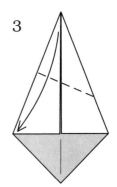

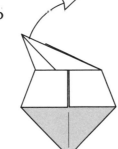

Unfold.

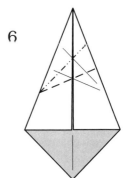

Repeat steps 3–5 in the other direction.

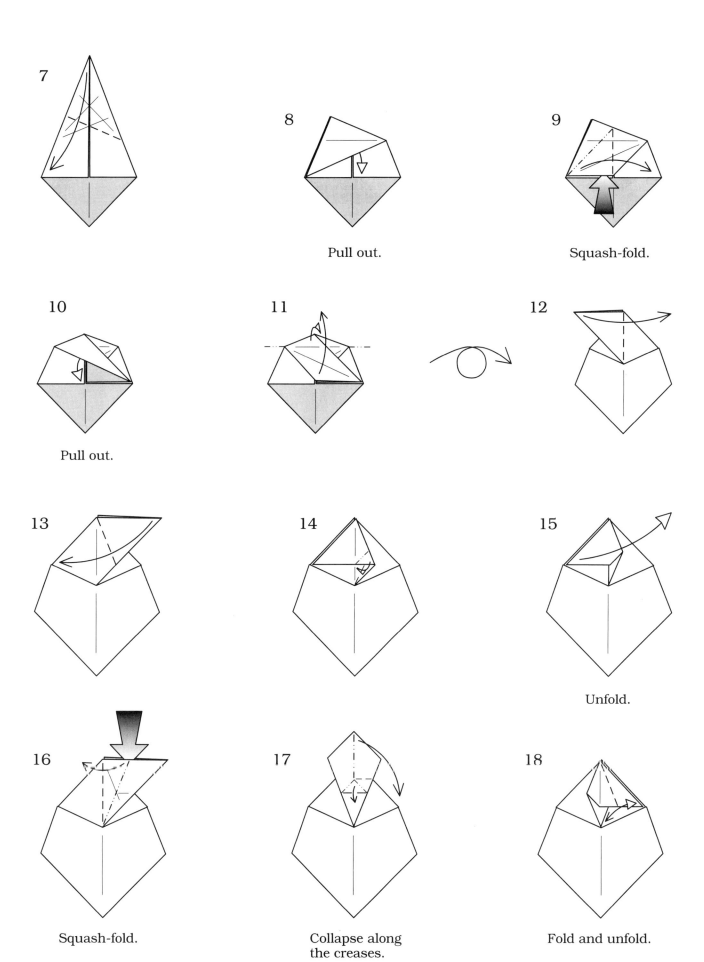

7

8

Pull out.

9

Squash-fold.

10

Pull out.

11

12

13

14

15

Unfold.

16

Squash-fold.

17

Collapse along
the creases.

18

Fold and unfold.

19

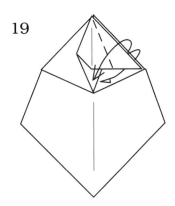

Outside-reverse-fold.

20

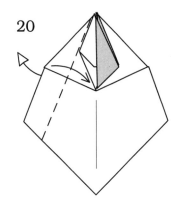

21

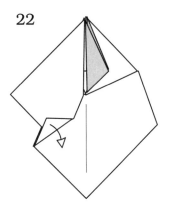

22

Unfold.

23

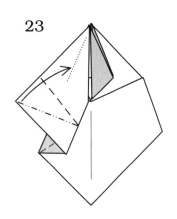

Squash-fold.

24

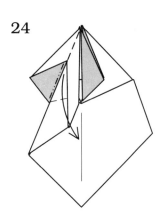

Squash-fold.

25

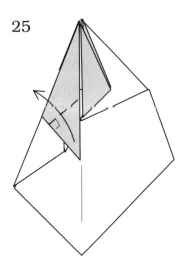

Note the right angle.

26

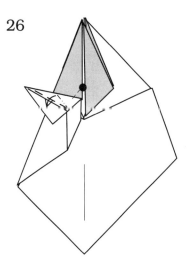

Squash-fold.

27

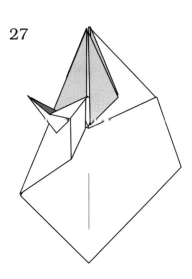

Tuck the dark paper inside.

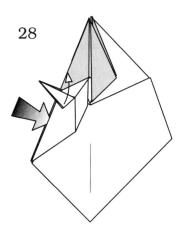

28

Unlock the paper.

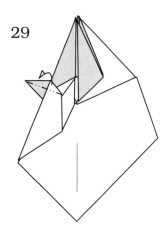

29

Tuck inside.

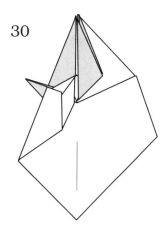

30

Repeat steps 20–29
on the right.

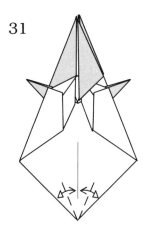

31

Kite-fold and unfold.

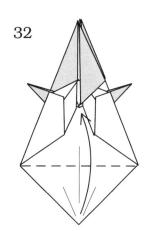

32

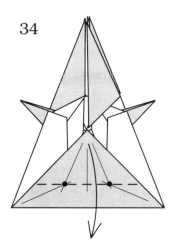

33

Fold and unfold.

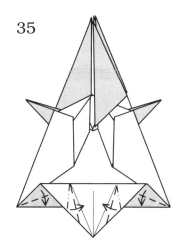

34

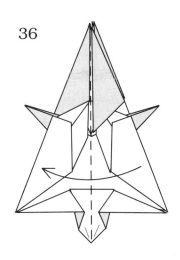

35

Squash folds.

36

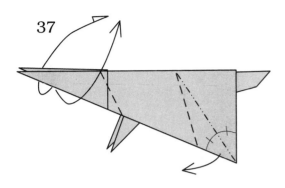

37

Outside-reverse-fold the
head. Crimp-fold the hind
legs. Note the bisection.

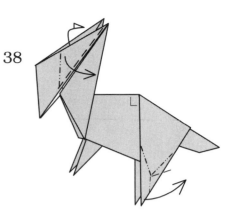

38

Crimp-fold at the head.
Double-rabbit-ear the
legs. Repeat behind.

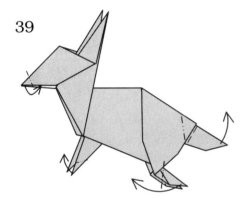

39

Reverse-fold the nose
and feet. Crimp-fold
the tail. Repeat behind.

40

Shape the nose, head
and open the ears.
Make the body round.

41

Rabbit

Squirrel

The squirrel was designed to have a large fluffy tail. The corners become the hind legs and tail, and one is hidden in the head.

1

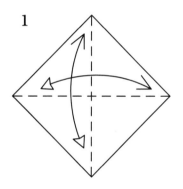

Fold and unfold.

2

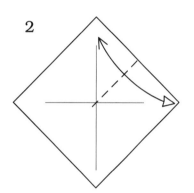

Fold and unfold.

3

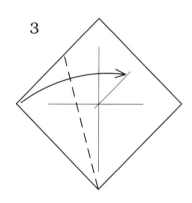

Fold the corner to the line.

4

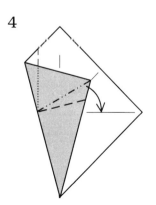

Fold to the crease.

5

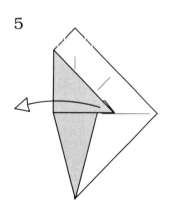

Unfold.

6

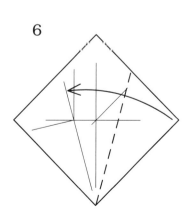

Fold to the crease.

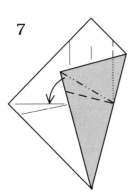

7

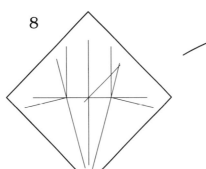

8

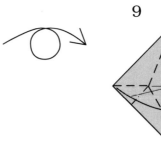

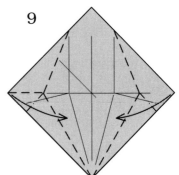

9

Repeat steps 4–5
on the right.

Rabbit ears.

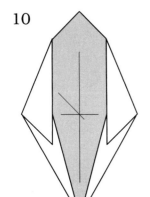

10

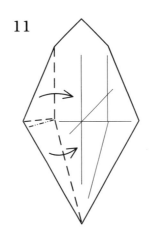

11

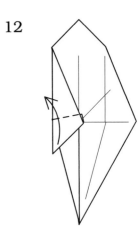

12

Rabbit-ear.

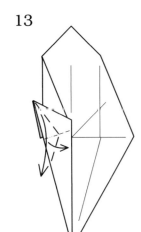

13

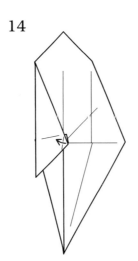

14

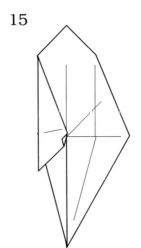

15

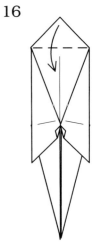

16

Repeat steps 11–14
on the right.

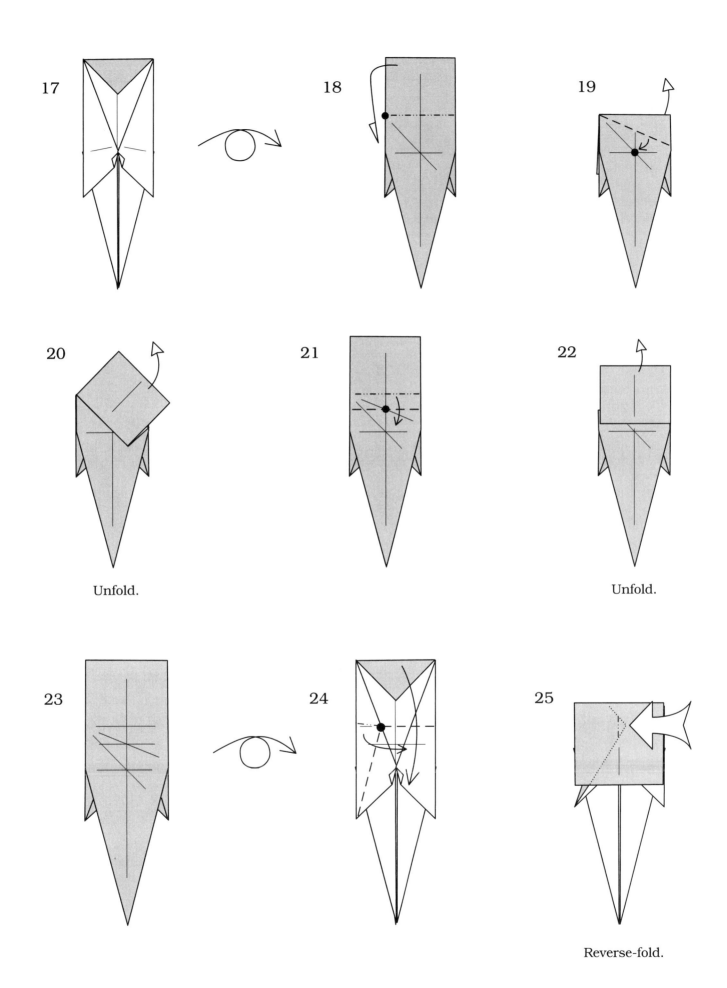

17

18

19

20

Unfold.

21

22

Unfold.

23

24

25

Reverse-fold.

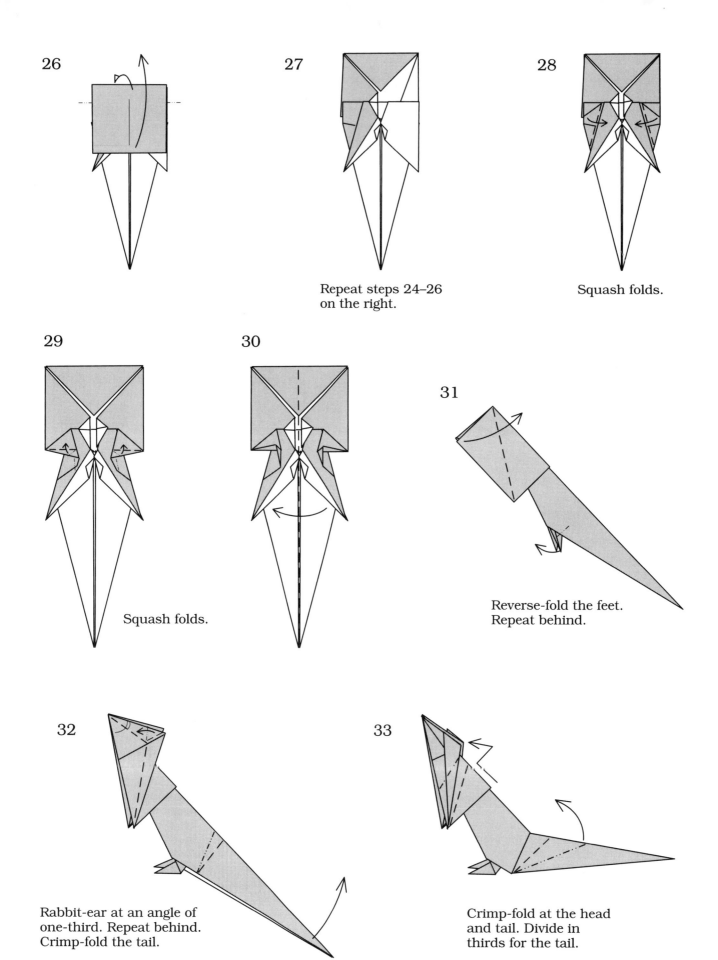

26

27 Repeat steps 24–26
on the right.

28 Squash folds.

29 Squash folds.

30

31 Reverse-fold the feet.
Repeat behind.

32 Rabbit-ear at an angle of
one-third. Repeat behind.
Crimp-fold the tail.

33 Crimp-fold at the head
and tail. Divide in
thirds for the tail.

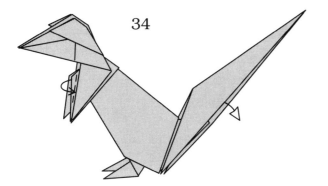

34

Tuck inside at the arms. Pull out
from the tail. Repeat behind.

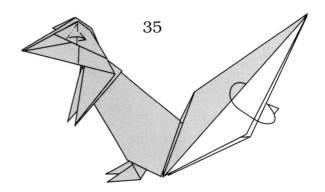

35

Squash-fold the ears. Fold the white
paper inside the tail. Repeat behind.

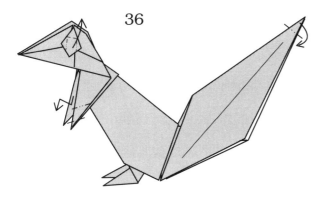

36

Petal-fold the ears. Crimp-fold
the arms. Repeat behind.
Reverse-fold the tip of the tail.

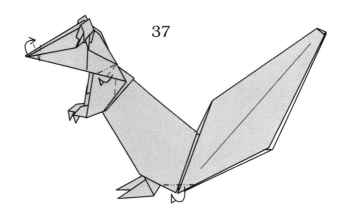

37

Repeat behind.

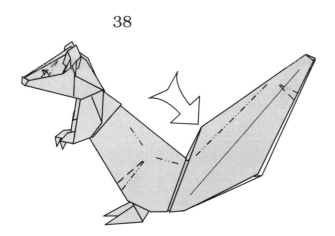

38

Repeat behind.

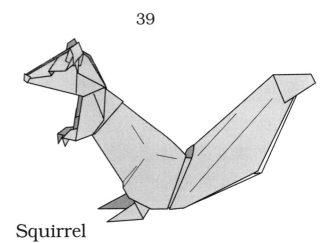

39

Squirrel

Horse

The folding for the horse features a new base, step 19, to allow for efficient use of the paper for making a seamless closed back. The corners are used for the head, tail, and front legs. The height of the horse is determined in just a few steps—see step 4. A few other animals—bear, bison, anteater, and lion—use variations of this structure.

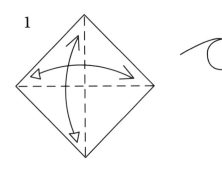

1

Fold and unfold.

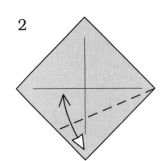

2

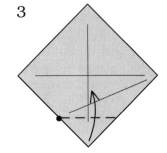

3

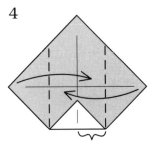

4

This shows the height of the horse to the top of its back (minus leg detail).

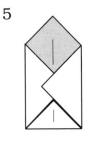

5

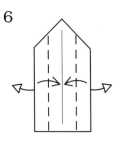

6

7

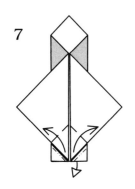

8

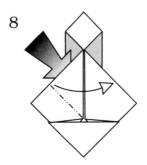

Pull out and rotate.

9

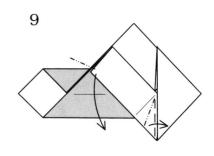

Squash-fold.

10

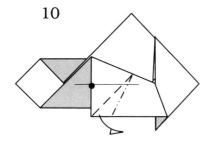

Squash-fold.

11

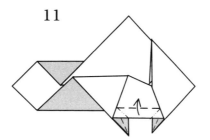

Petal-fold.

12

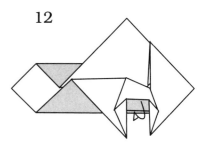

Fold behind.

13

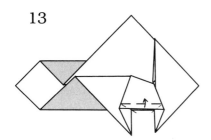

Spread squash folds.

14

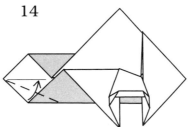

15

16

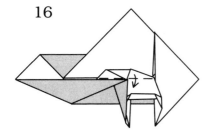

17

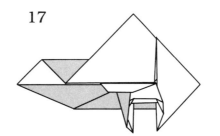

Repeat steps 8–16
on the upper part.

18

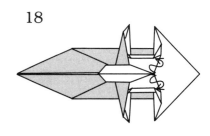

Bring the paper to the front.

19

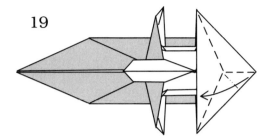

Rabbit-ear.

20

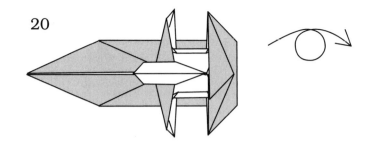

21

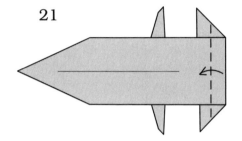

22

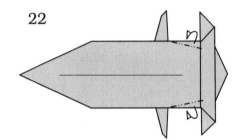

23

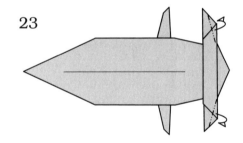

Tuck inside.

24

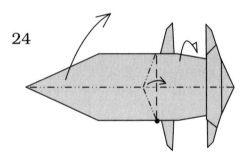

Note the dot is a little
to the left of the leg.

25

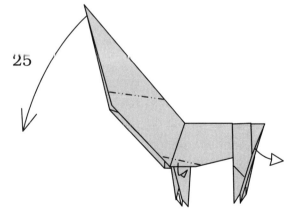

Reverse-fold the head, tuck inside at the front
legs, and pull out the tail. Repeat behind.

26

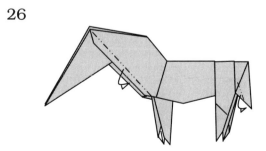

Squash-fold the tail.
Repeat behind.

27

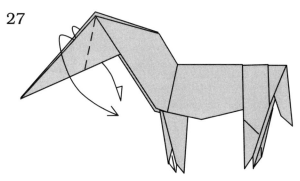

Outside-reverse-fold.

28

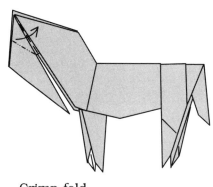

Crimp-fold.

29

Reverse-fold the tip of the head, and crimp-fold the hind hooves. Repeat behind.

30

Outside-reverse-fold the nose.

31

Three dimensional folding. Repeat behind.

32

Horse

Bear

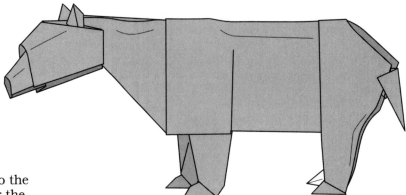

The structure for the bear is similar to the horse. Since less paper is required for the neck and head, the height of the bear is a little greater than that of the horse. Its height is determined in step 6, where the corner is folded up slightly higher than that of the horse. Compare bases—step 19 of both models.

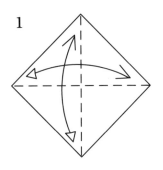

1

Fold and unfold.

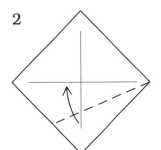

2

Crease lightly.

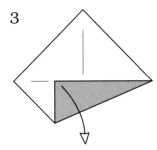

3

Unfold.

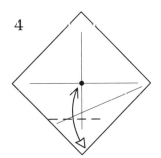

4

Fold up to the center and unfold. Crease lightly and only on the left side.

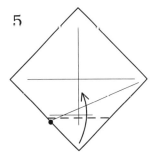

5

Fold up so the dot meets the line above it.

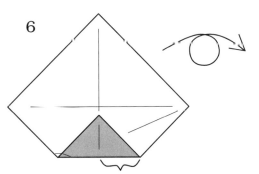

6

Height of the back (minus leg detail).

7

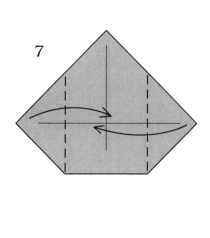

8

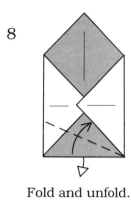

Fold and unfold.

9

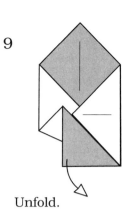

Unfold.

10

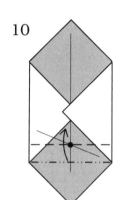

11

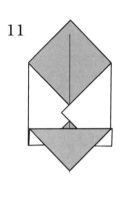

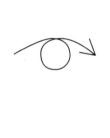

12

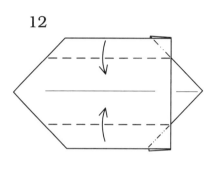

Squash folds.

13

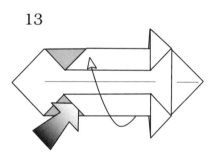

Pull out the corner.

14

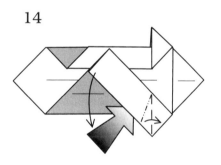

Squash-fold.

15

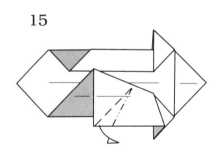

Squash-fold.

16

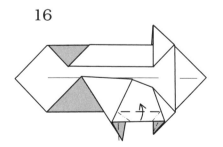

Petal-fold.

17

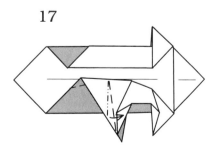

Squash-fold.

18

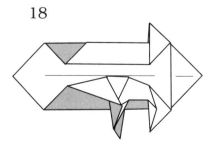

Repeat steps 13–17
on the top.

19

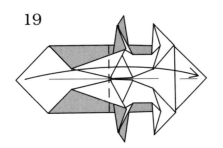

20

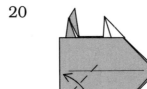

Fold and unfold.

21

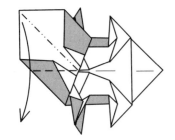

22

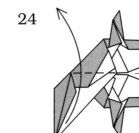

Squash-fold.

23

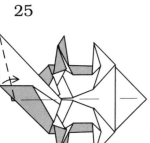

24

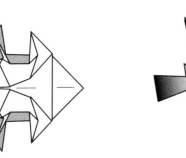

25

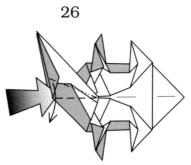

26

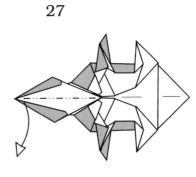

Squash-fold.

27

Unfold.

28

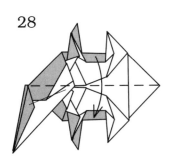

29

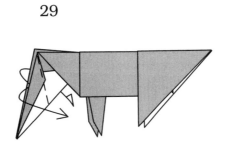

Outside-reverse-fold.

30

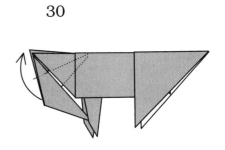

Crimp-fold.

31

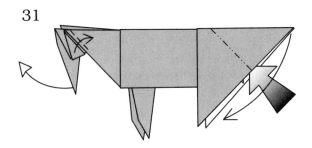

Pull the head while covering the ear.
Repeat behind. Reverse-fold at the tail.

32

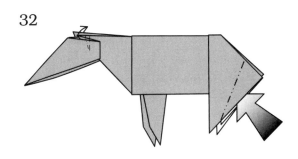

Fold the ear and reverse-fold
at the tail. Repeat behind.

33

Crimp-fold the head and
reverse-fold the tail.

34

Repeat behind.

35

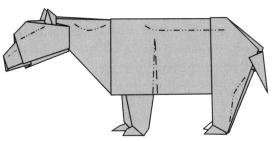

Shape the bear. Repeat behind.

36

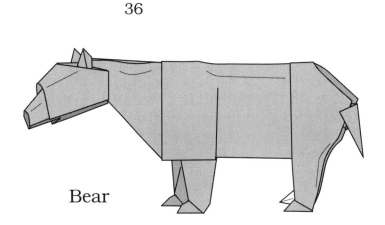

Bear

Bison

The bison's massive body is represented here. It uses a base similar to the bear.

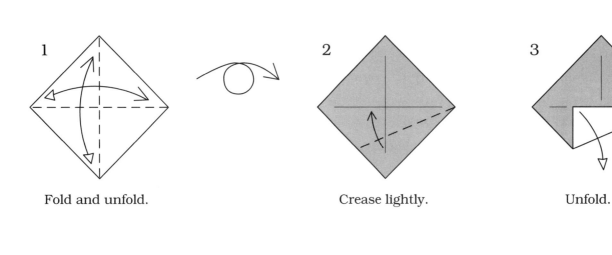

1

Fold and unfold.

2

Crease lightly.

3

Unfold.

4

Fold up to the center and unfold. Crease lightly and only on the left side.

5

Fold up so the dot meets the line above it.

6

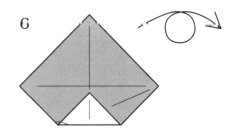

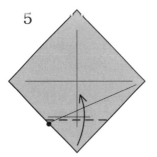

7

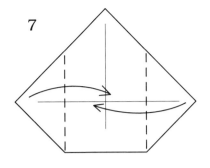

8

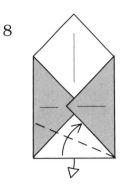

Fold and unfold.

9

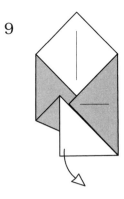

Unfold.

10

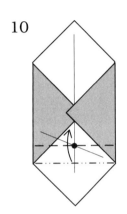

11

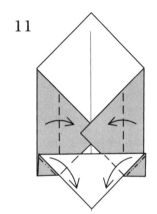

Squash folds. Rotate.

12

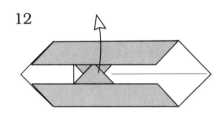

Pull out.

13

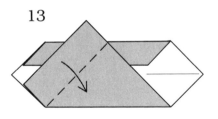

14

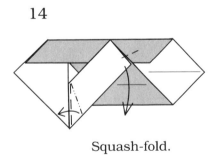

Squash-fold.

15

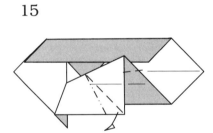

Squash-fold the front leg.

16

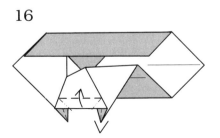

Note the "V" orientation of
the front leg. Petal-fold.

17

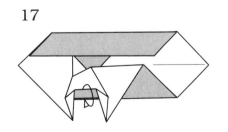

Fold behind.

18

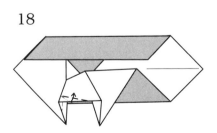

Spread-squash-fold.

19

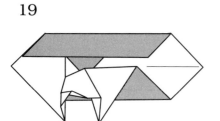

Repeat steps 12–18 on the top.

20

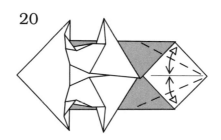

Fold and unfold.

21

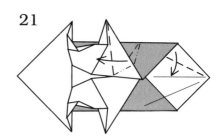

22

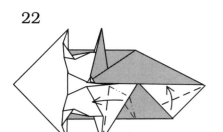

23

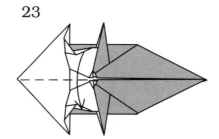

24

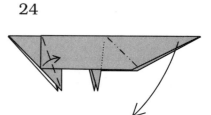

Reverse-fold the head. Repeat behind at the back.

25

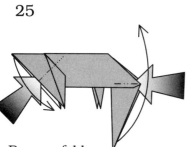

Reverse folds.

26

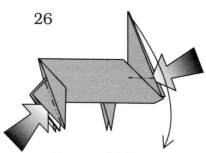

Reverse folds. Repeat behind.

27

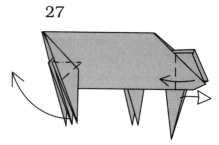

Crimp-fold the tail. Pull out the head.

28

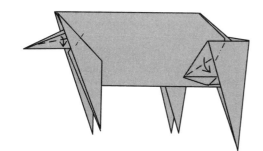

Repeat behind.

29

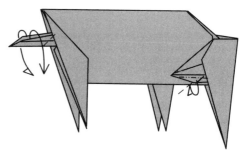

Outside-reverse-fold the tail. Push in at the horn and repeat behind.

30

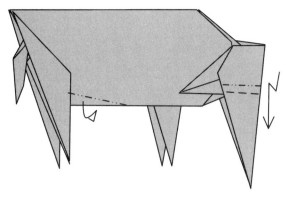

Crimp-fold the head. Repeat
behind for the body.

31

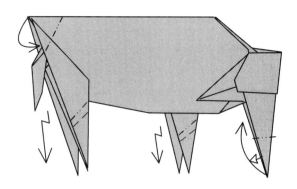

Spread the paper while reverse folding
up at the head. Repeat behind.

32

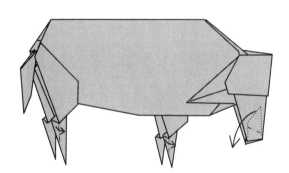

Repeat on the underside of
each leg. Repeat behind.

33

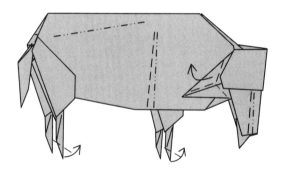

Curl the horns. Make the body
three-dimensional. Repeat behind.

34

Bison

Anteater

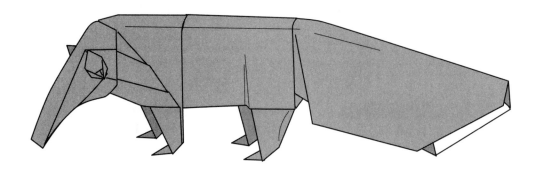

To create the large tail, the anteater uses a
variation of the structure used for the bison.
Compare steps 23 of these two animals.

1

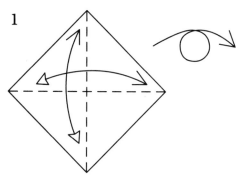

Fold and unfold
along the diagonals.

2

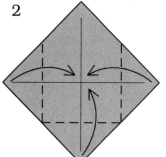

3

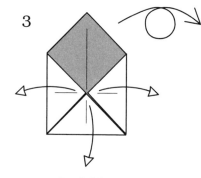

Unfold.

4

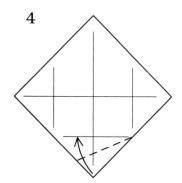

5

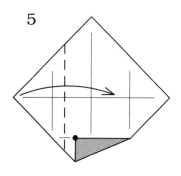

6

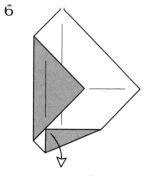

Unfold.

7

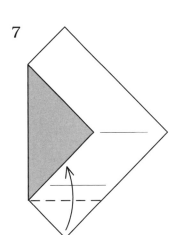

8

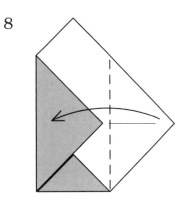

9

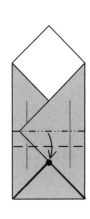

10

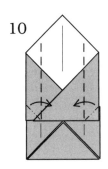

Squash folds.

11

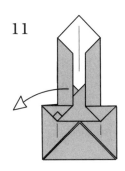

Unfold almost
everything.

12

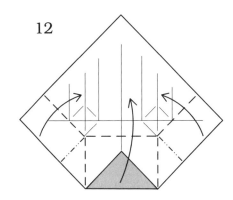

13

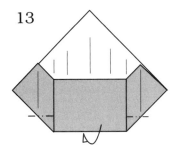

Fold along the crease.

14

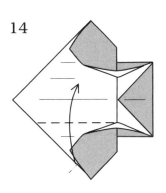

The model is three-dimensional.
Do not flatten.

15

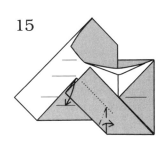

16

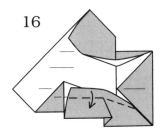

17

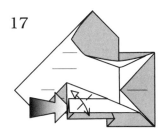

Fold and unfold.

18

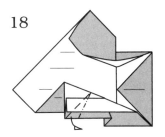

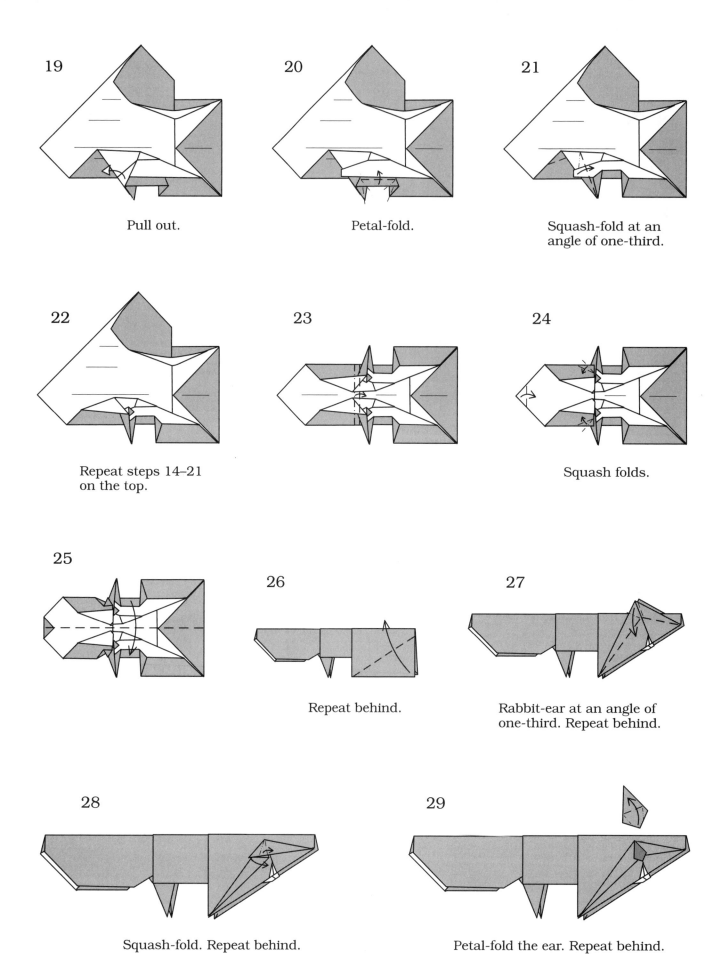

19

Pull out.

20

Petal-fold.

21

Squash-fold at an
angle of one-third.

22

Repeat steps 14–21
on the top.

23

24

Squash folds.

25

26

Repeat behind.

27

Rabbit-ear at an angle of
one-third. Repeat behind.

28

Squash-fold. Repeat behind.

29

Petal-fold the ear. Repeat behind.

30

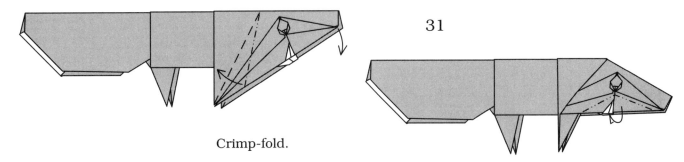

Crimp-fold.

31

Repeat behind.

32

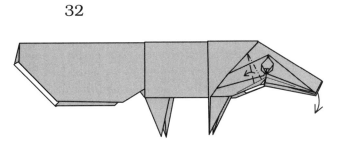

The head is three-dimensional.

33

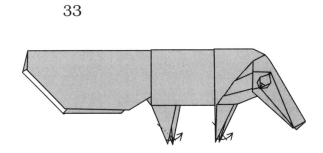

The top of the head is three-dimensional.
Reverse-fold the feet. Repeat behind.

34

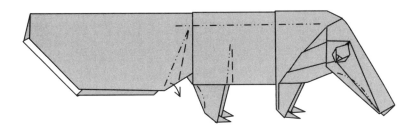

Shape the anteater.

35

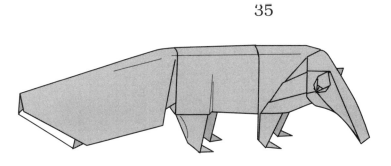

Anteater

Crane

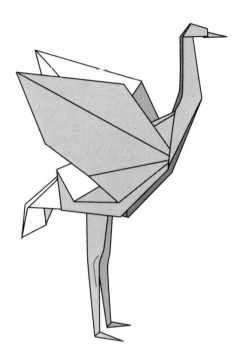

Creating long legs, wings, and neck is always a challenge. The head comes from an off-center location (see step 2). The legs and wings come from the four corners. Step 11 resembles a waterbomb base on one side and a preliminary fold on the other.

1

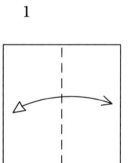

Fold and unfold.

2

The location of the head is at the ◆.

3

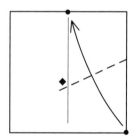

4

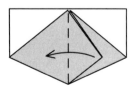

5

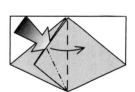

6

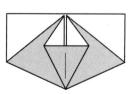

Turn over and rotate.

7

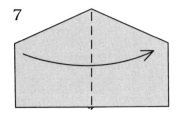

8

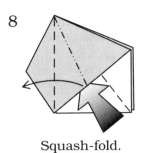

Squash-fold.

9

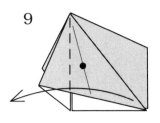

Note the crease
with the dot.

10

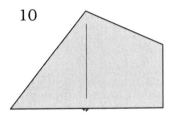

Repeat steps 7–9
on the right.

11

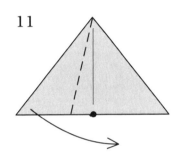

Fold along the crease shown
in step 9. The dot shown
here will be used in step 12.

12

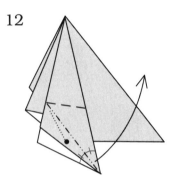

Bisect the angle for
this squash-fold.

13

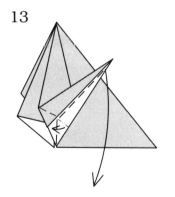

Rabbit-ear.

14

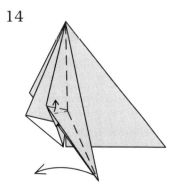

15

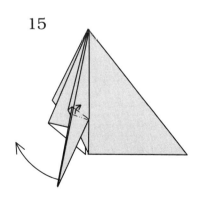

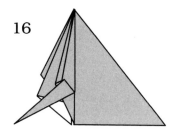

16

Repeat steps 11–15
on the right.

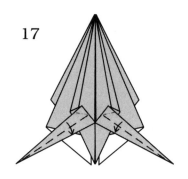

17

Fold all the layers.

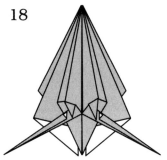

18

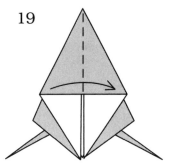

19

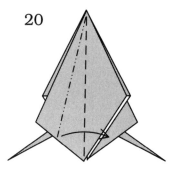

20

Squash-fold.

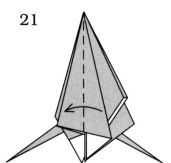

21

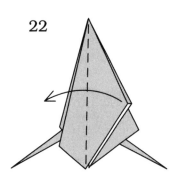

22

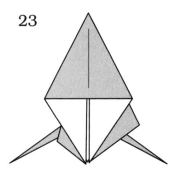

23

Repeat steps 19–22
on the right.

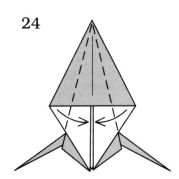

24

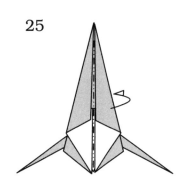

25

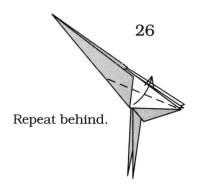

26

Repeat behind.

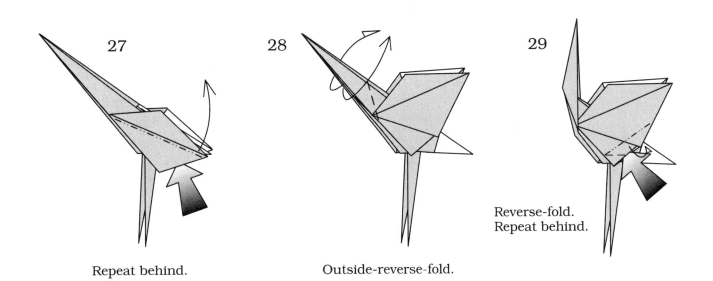

27

Repeat behind.

28

Outside-reverse-fold.

29

Reverse-fold.
Repeat behind.

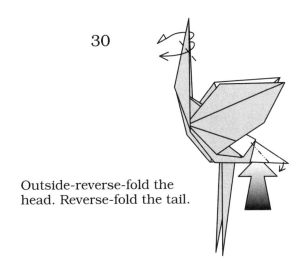

30

Outside-reverse-fold the
head. Reverse-fold the tail.

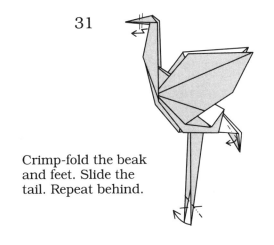

31

Crimp-fold the beak
and feet. Slide the
tail. Repeat behind.

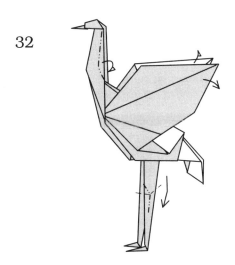

32

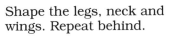

Shape the legs, neck and
wings. Repeat behind.

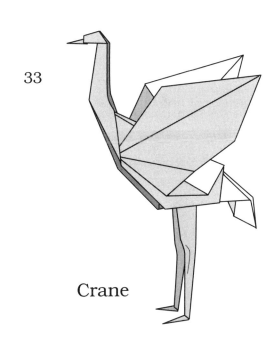

33

Crane

Ibis

It is interesting to give the added detail of the toes. As you are shaping them in step 47, you do not really need to follow the directions completely, as any method of forming the toes will do. The corners are used for the head, sets of toes, and pair of wings.

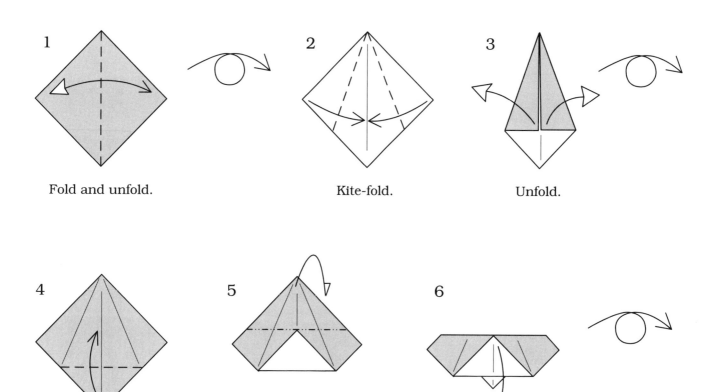

1

Fold and unfold.

2

Kite-fold.

3

Unfold.

4

5

6

Unfold.

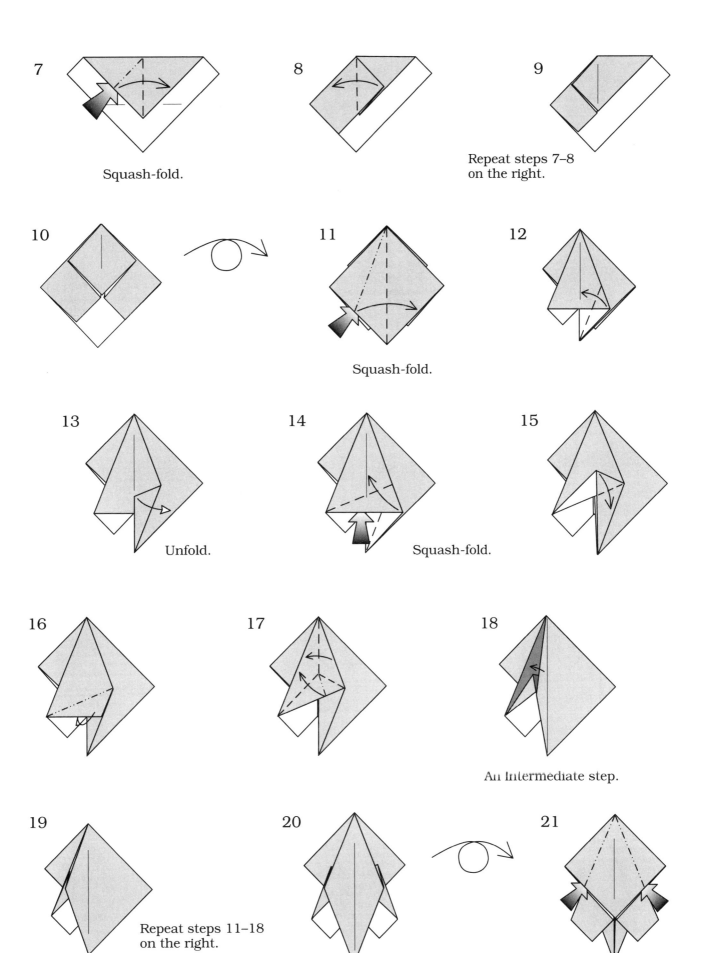

7

Squash-fold.

8

9

Repeat steps 7–8
on the right.

10

11

Squash-fold.

12

13

Unfold.

14

Squash-fold.

15

16

17

18

An intermediate step.

19

Repeat steps 11–18
on the right.

20

21

Ibis 75

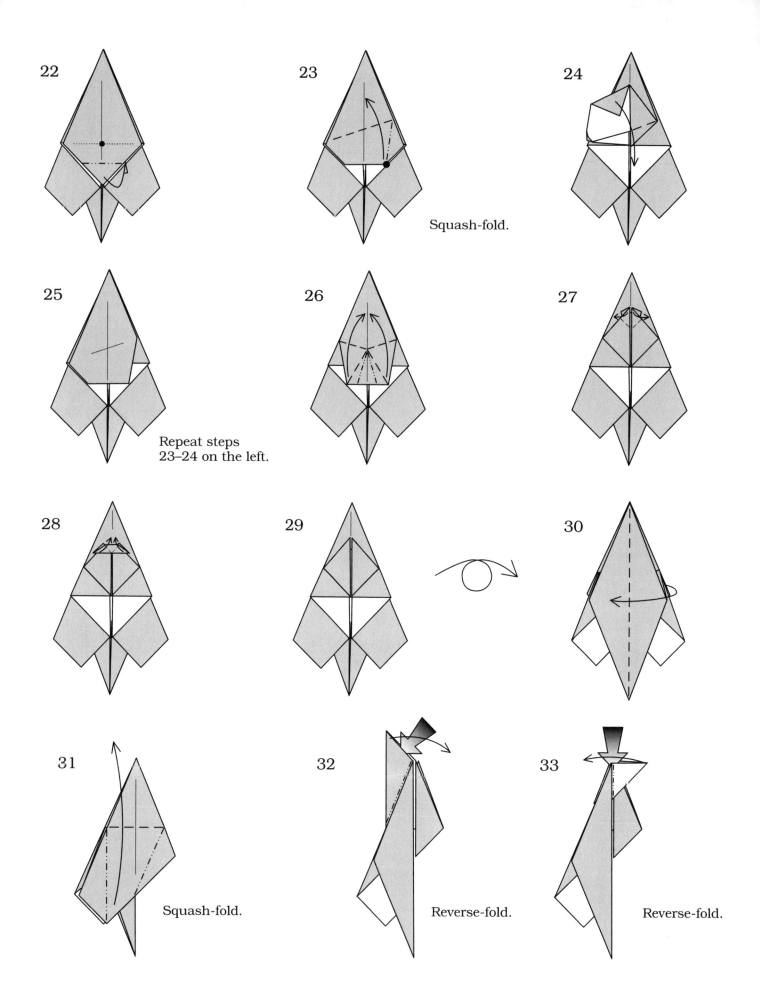

22

23

Squash-fold.

24

25

Repeat steps
23–24 on the left.

26

27

28

29

30

31

Squash-fold.

32

Reverse-fold.

33

Reverse-fold.

34

Reverse-fold.

35

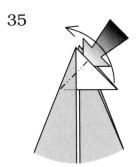

Reverse-fold.

36

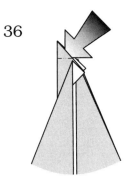

Reverse-fold.

37

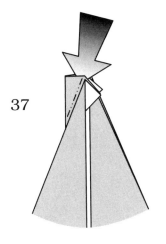

Reverse-fold.

38

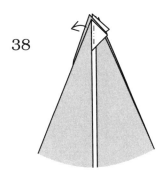

Three reverse folds.

39

Three reverse folds.

40

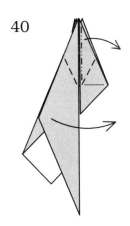

41

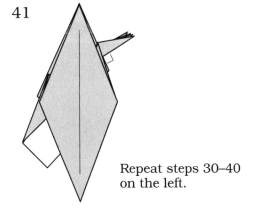

Repeat steps 30–40
on the left.

42

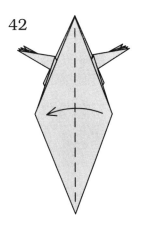

43

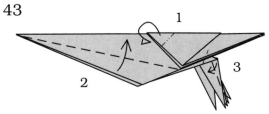

Repeat behind.

44

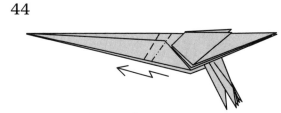

Crimp-fold.

45

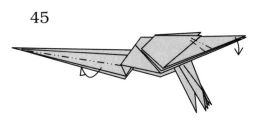

Crimp-fold the tail. Repeat
behind for the neck.

46

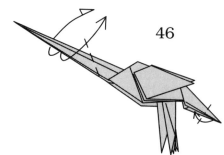

Reverse-fold the tail.
Outside-reverse-fold the neck.

47

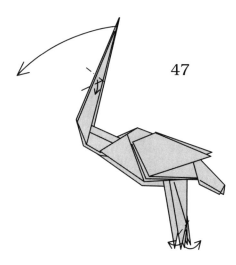

Spread while folding the head. For
the toes, fold the first in front, the
next one to the back, then fold two
together behind. Repeat behind.
The bird can stand.

48

Form the head with
crimp folds. Thin the
leg and repeat behind.

49

Ibis

Kangaroo

The kangaroo, with its ears and short arms at the top, and long legs and tail on the bottom present interesting challenges for the designer. I have fashioned some form of a stretched bird base, see step 19, to achieve this result. The corners are used for the head, tail, and hind legs.

1
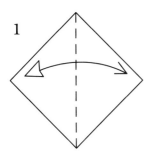
Fold and unfold.

2
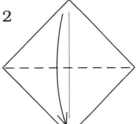

3
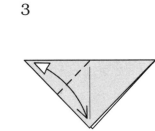
Fold and unfold.

4
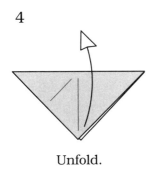
Unfold.

5
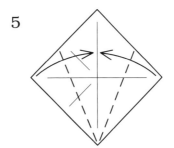

6
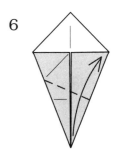

7

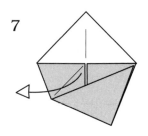

Unfold everything.

8

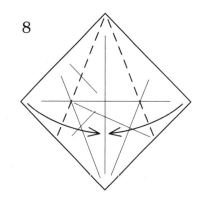

9

10

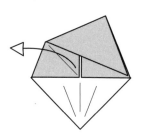

Unfold everything.

11

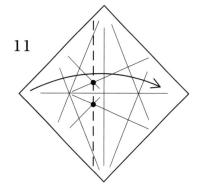

Rotate.

12

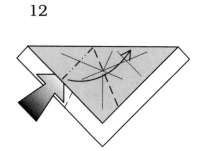

Squash-fold.

13

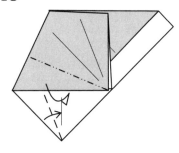

14

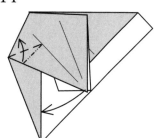

15

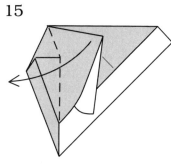

This is three-dimensional.

16

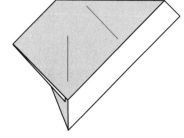

Repeat steps 12–15
on the right.

17

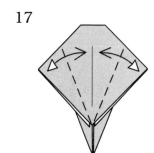

Fold and unfold.

18

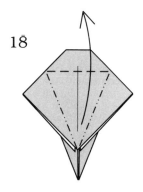

Petal-fold.

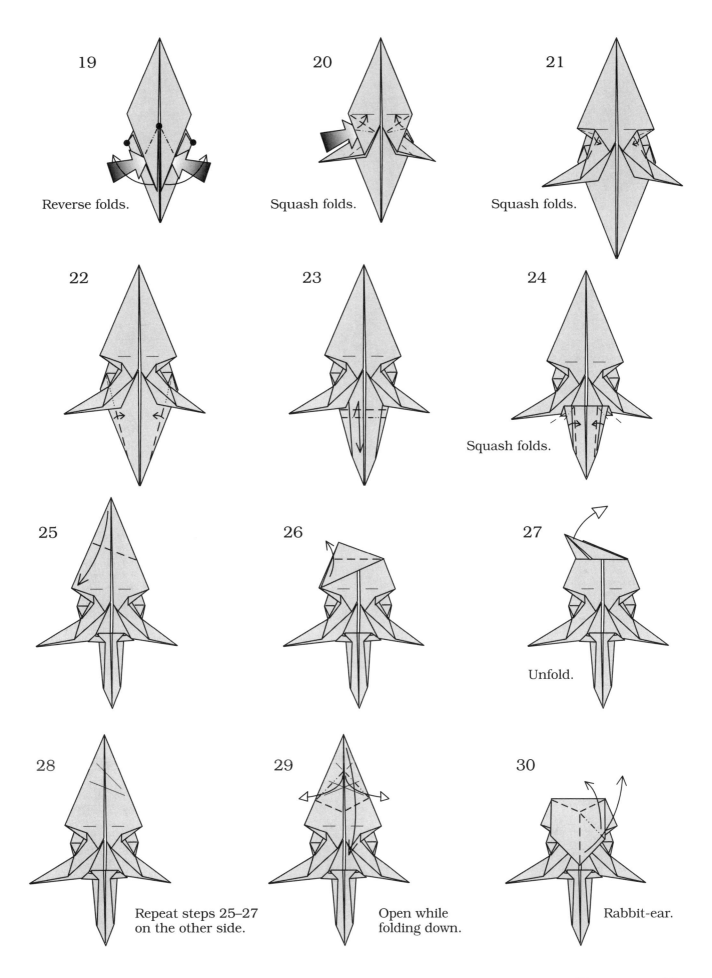

19

Reverse folds.

20

Squash folds.

21

Squash folds.

22

23

24

Squash folds.

25

26

27

Unfold.

28

Repeat steps 25–27
on the other side.

29

Open while
folding down.

30

Rabbit-ear.

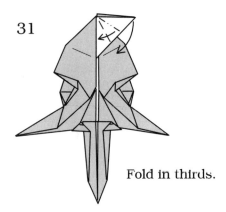

31

Fold in thirds.

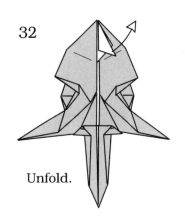

32

Unfold.

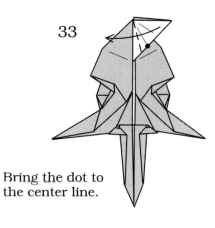

33

Bring the dot to
the center line.

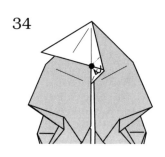

34

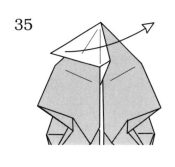

35

Unfold.

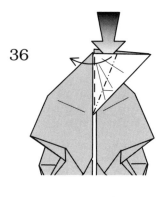

36

Squash-fold.

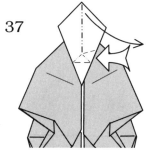

37

Fold along
the creases.

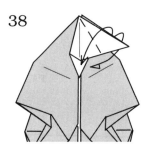

38

Outside-reverse-fold.

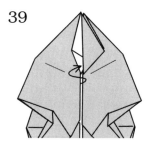

39

Cover the white paper
and repeat on the right.

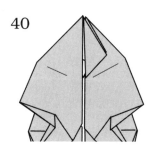

40

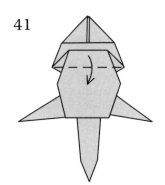

41

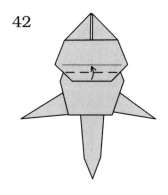

42

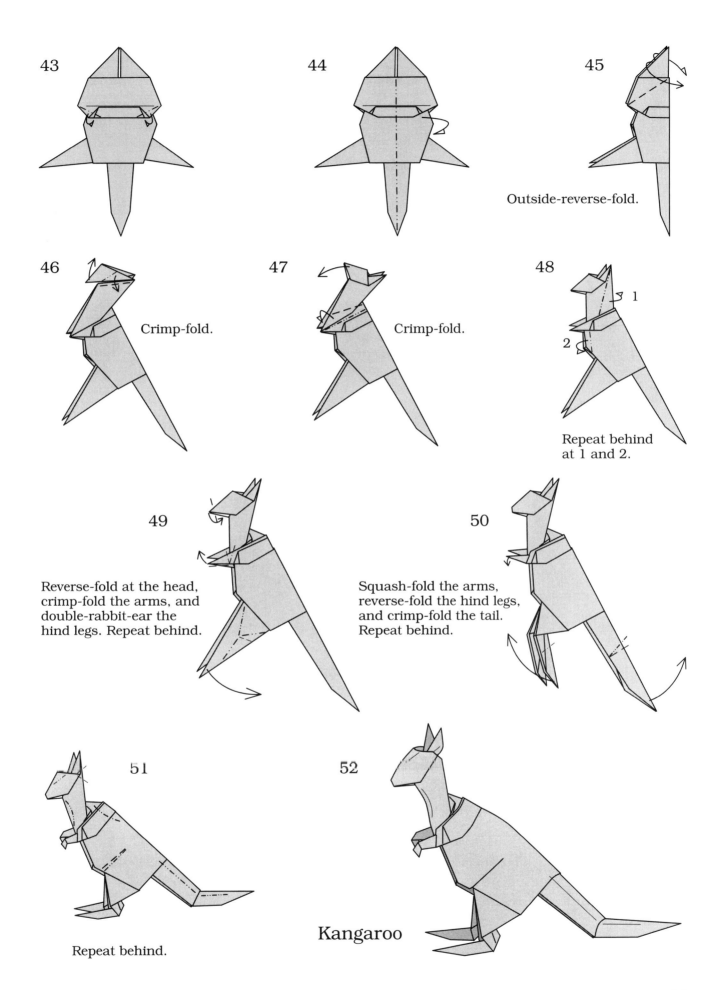

43

44

45

Outside-reverse-fold.

46

Crimp-fold.

47

Crimp-fold.

48

1

2

Repeat behind
at 1 and 2.

49

Reverse-fold at the head,
crimp-fold the arms, and
double-rabbit-ear the
hind legs. Repeat behind.

50

Squash-fold the arms,
reverse-fold the hind legs,
and crimp-fold the tail.
Repeat behind.

51

Repeat behind.

52

Kangaroo

Coyote

For this howling coyote, nearly half the paper is used for the neck and head. The corners become the lower jaw, tail, and front legs.

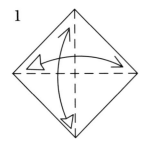

1

Fold and unfold along the diagonals.

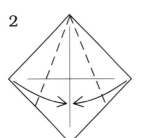

2

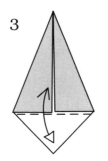

3

Fold and unfold.

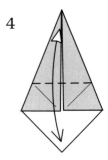

4

Fold and unfold.

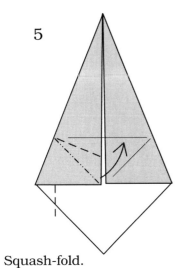

5

Squash-fold.

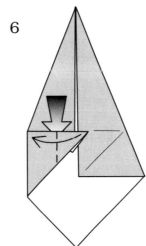

6

Squash-fold.

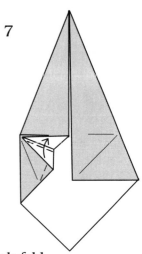

7

Squash-fold.

8

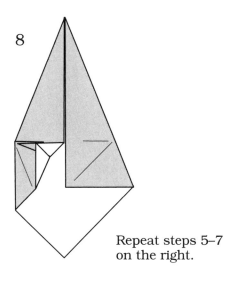

Repeat steps 5–7 on the right.

9

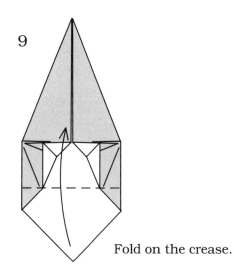

Fold on the crease.

10

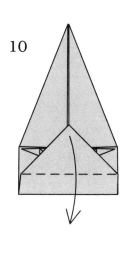

11

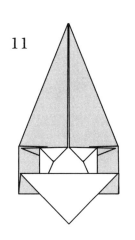

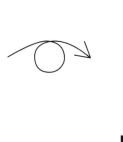

12

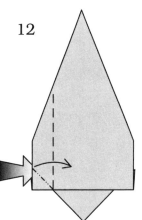

Squash-fold.

13

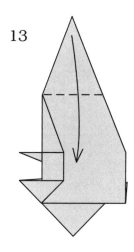

14

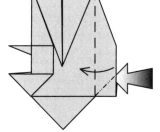

Squash-fold.

15

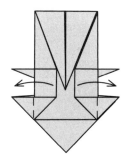

16

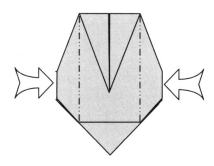

Sink.

Coyote 85

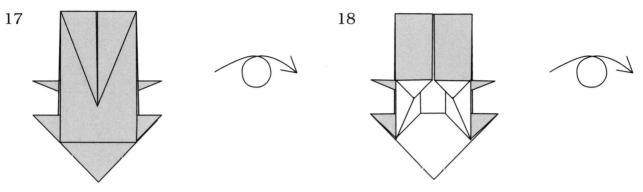

17

Turn over to see the results of
the sink fold on both sides.

18

19

20

21

Unfold.

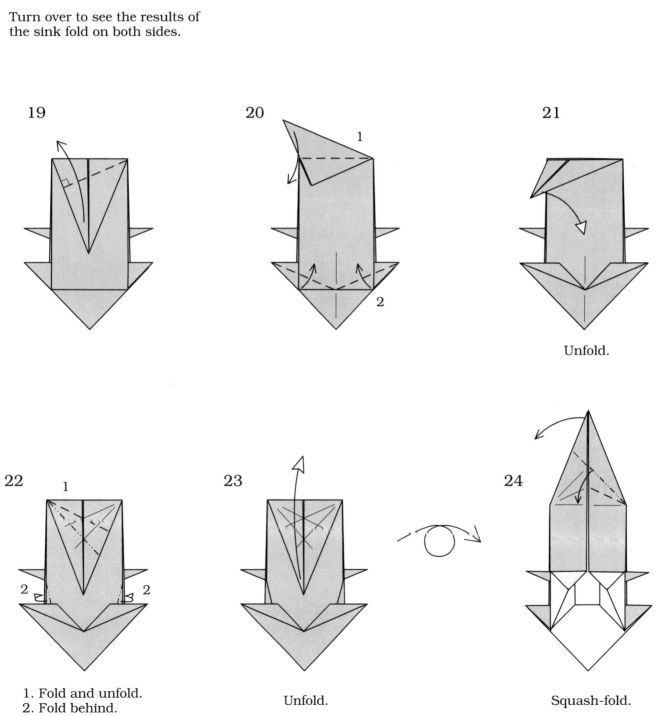

22

1. Fold and unfold.
2. Fold behind.

23

Unfold.

24

Squash-fold.

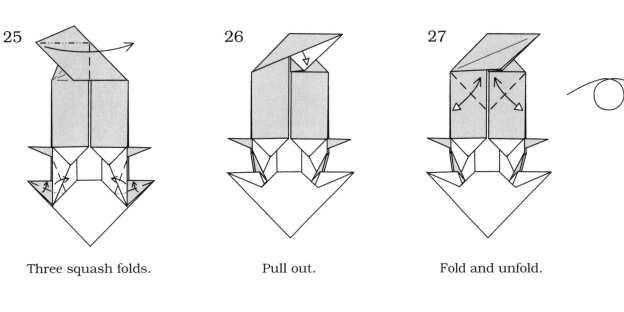

25   Three squash folds.

26   Pull out.

27   Fold and unfold.

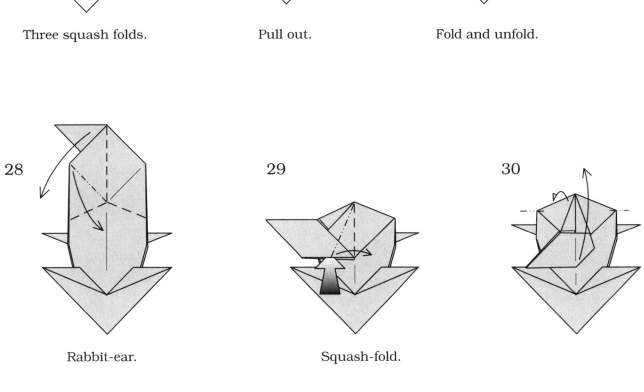

28   Rabbit-ear.

29   Squash-fold.

30

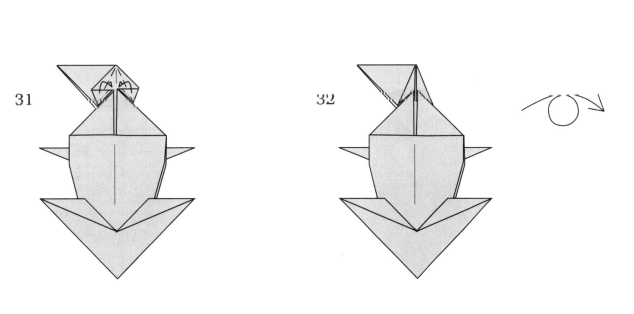

31

32

33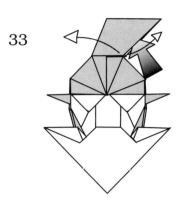

Open.

34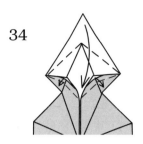

This is three-dimensional.
Flatten.

35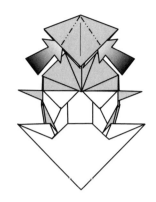

Reverse folds.

36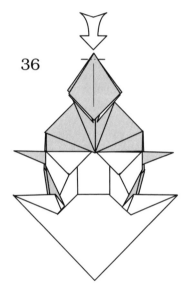

Sink.

37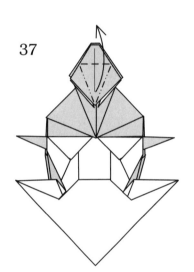

Petal-fold.

38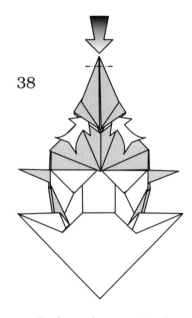

Sink at the top. Push
in the white paper.

39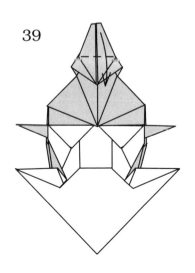

40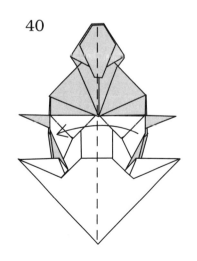

41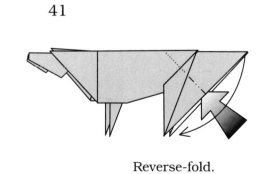

Reverse-fold.

42

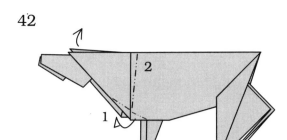

Stretch and curl behind at 1 and repeat behind. Then change the angle of the neck at 2. This gives a rounder neck.

43

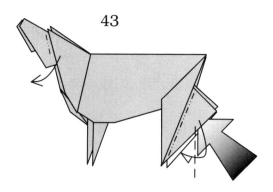

Reverse folds.
Repeat behind.

44

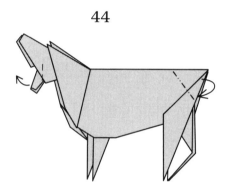

Outside-reverse-fold the jaw.
Reverse-fold at the back.

45

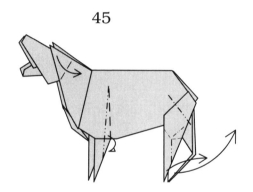

Repeat behind.

46

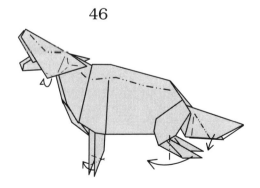

Repeat behind.

47

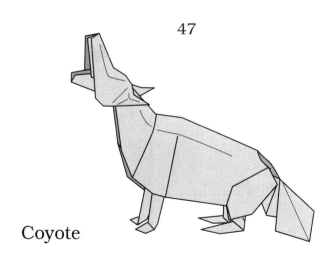

Coyote

African Elephant

This elephant, with only 40 steps, takes much fewer steps than any other detailed elephant I have designed. Several new techniques are used, such as the folds leading up to step 15, and the way in step 24 the legs and tusk are formed together. The corners are used for the head, tusks, and tail.

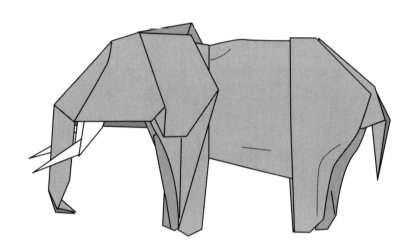

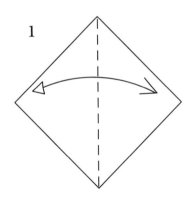

1

Fold and unfold.

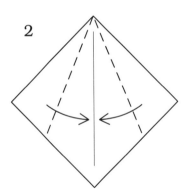

2

3

Fold and unfold.

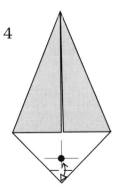

4

Fold and unfold.

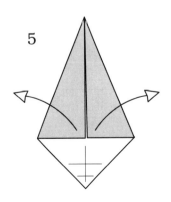

5

Unfold.

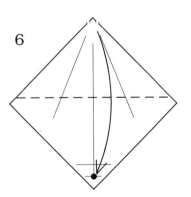

6

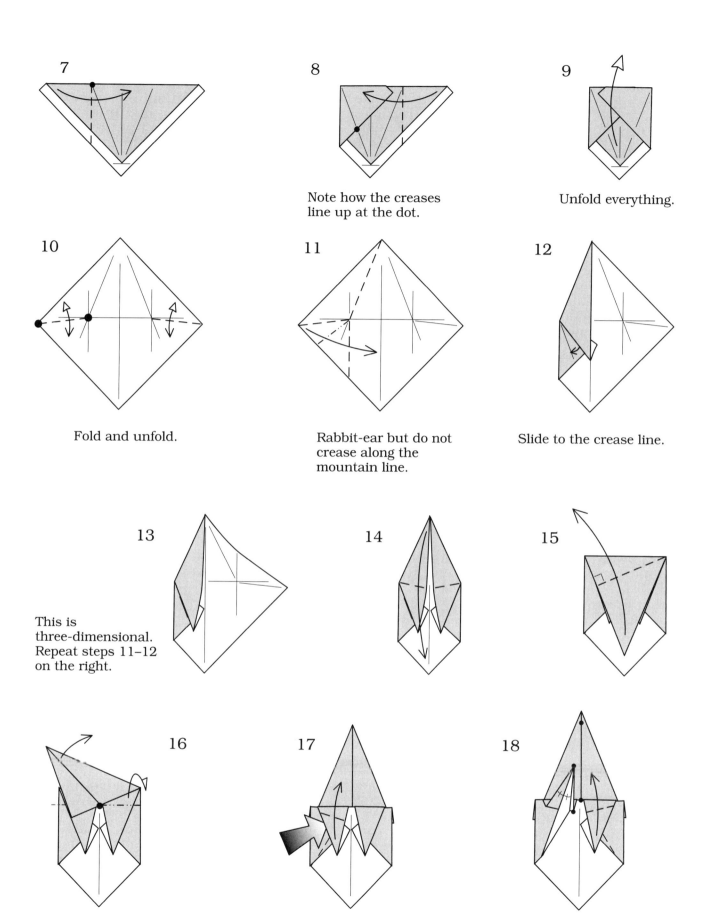

7

8

Note how the creases
line up at the dot.

9

Unfold everything.

10

Fold and unfold.

11

Rabbit-ear but do not
crease along the
mountain line.

12

Slide to the crease line.

13

This is
three-dimensional.
Repeat steps 11–12
on the right.

14

15

16

17

Squash-fold.

18

The two lines with the dots are
vertical, and the two angles are
the same. Squash-fold.

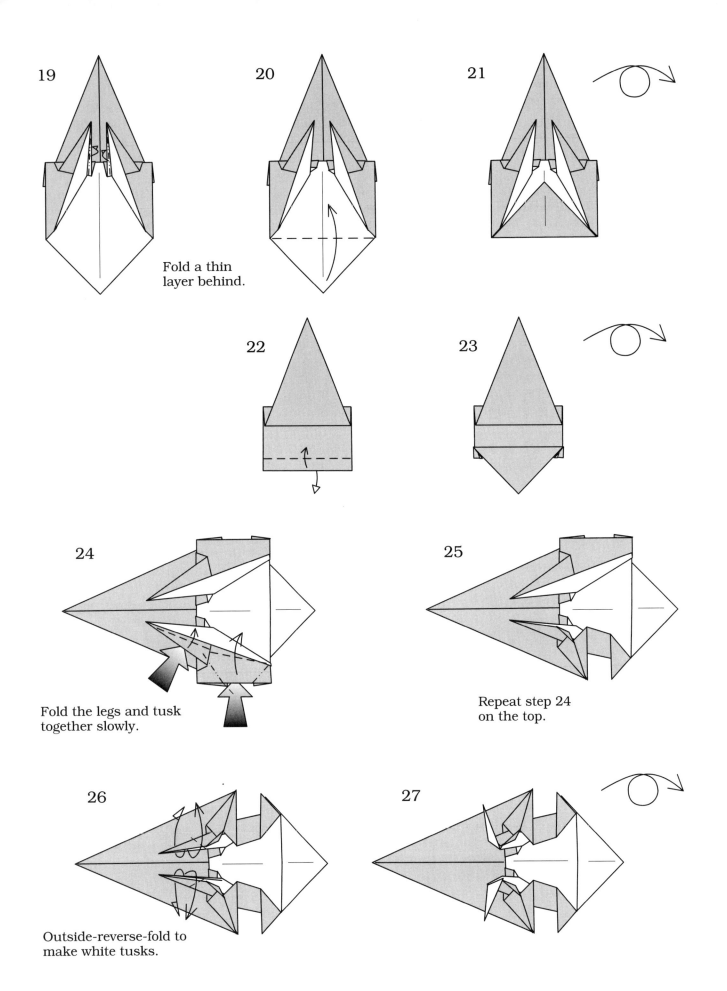

19

20

Fold a thin
layer behind.

21

22

23

24

Fold the legs and tusk
together slowly.

25

Repeat step 24
on the top.

26

Outside-reverse-fold to
make white tusks.

27

28

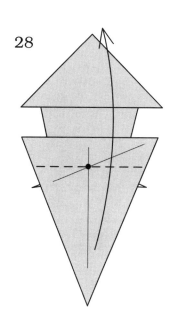

29

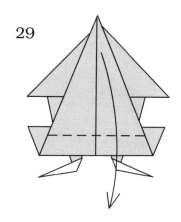

30

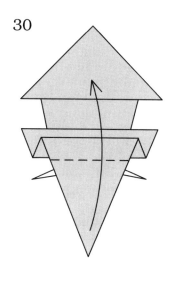

31

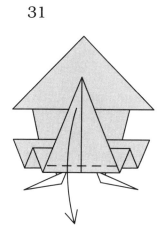

32

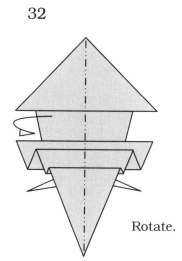

Rotate.

33

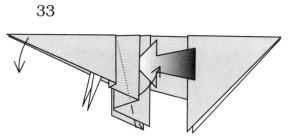

Slide the head.

34

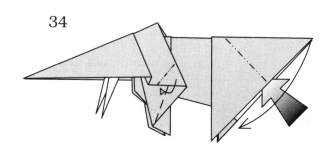

Repeat behind at the ears
and reverse-fold the tail.

35

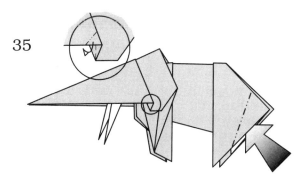

Fold in at the ears and reverse-fold
the tail. Repeat behind.

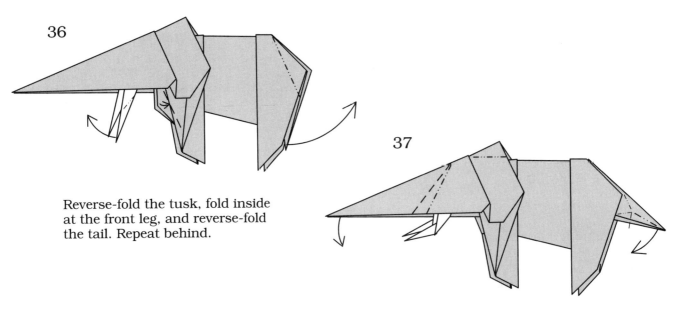

36

Reverse-fold the tusk, fold inside
at the front leg, and reverse-fold
the tail. Repeat behind.

37

Crimp-fold the trunk, reverse-fold the
ear, and double-rabbit-eat the tail.

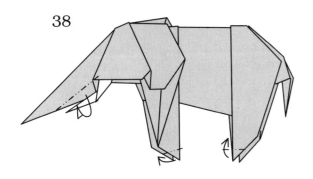

38

Repeat behind.

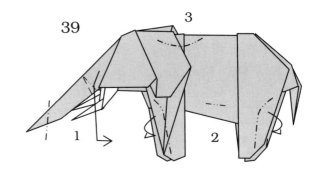

39

1. Shape the trunk.
2. Curve the legs. The lower part of
   the body will be lightly curved, too.
3. Push in at the top.

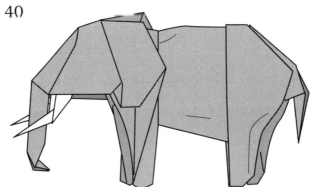

40

African Elephant

Lion

I took the head and mane from a previous lion design (from *African Animals in Origami*) and combined it with the seamless closed back of the bear to fashion this lion. The corners are used for the head and tail, and two are hidden in the front legs.

1

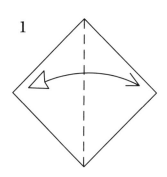

Fold and unfold.

2

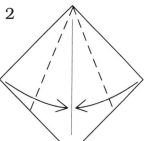

3

Fold and unfold.

4

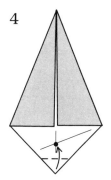

5

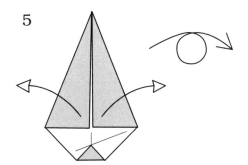

Unfold.

6

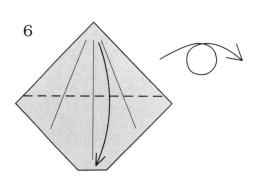

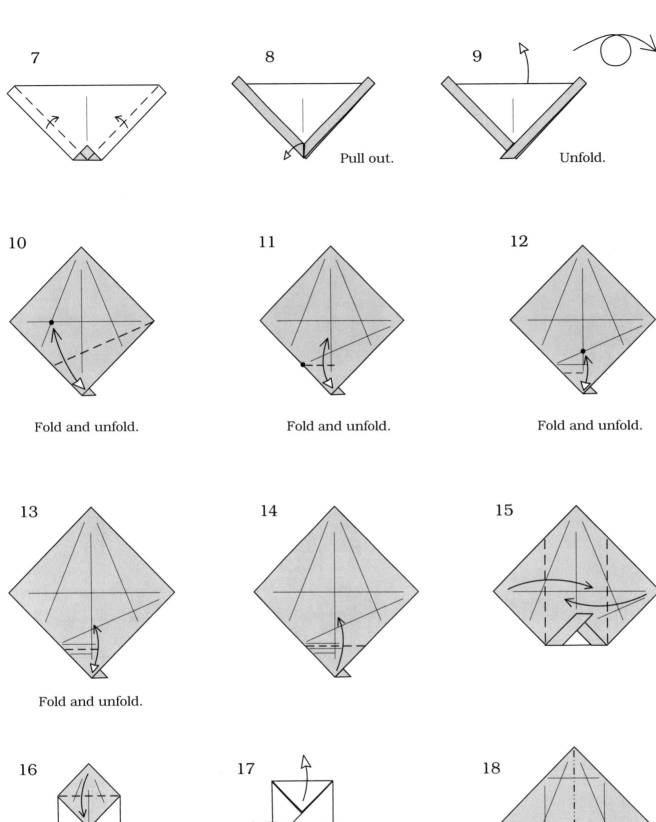

7

8

Pull out.

9

Unfold.

10

Fold and unfold.

11

Fold and unfold.

12

Fold and unfold.

13

Fold and unfold.

14

15

16

17

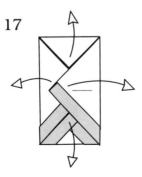

Unfold.

18

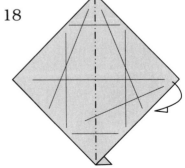

Mountain-fold and rotate.

19

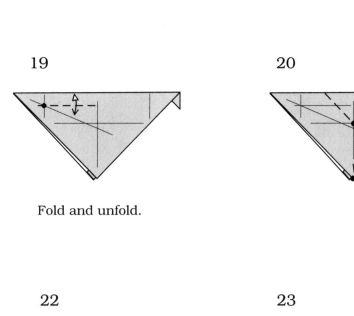

Fold and unfold.

20

21

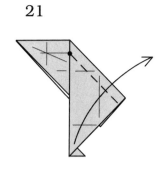

22

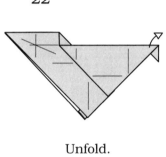

Unfold.

23

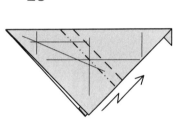

Crimp-fold.

24

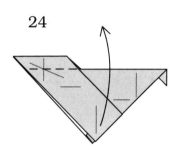

25

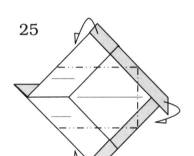

26

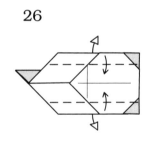

27

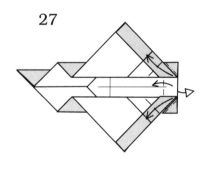

28

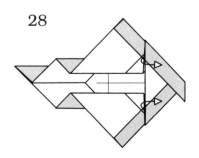

Pull out some paper.

29

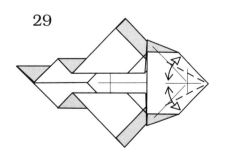

Fold and unfold.

30

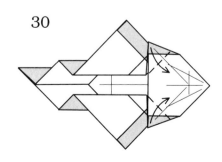

31

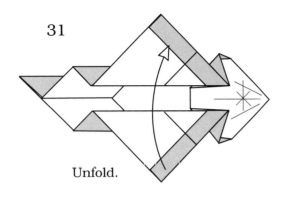

Unfold.

32

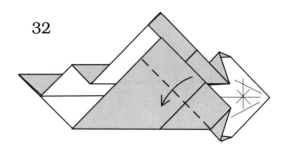

33

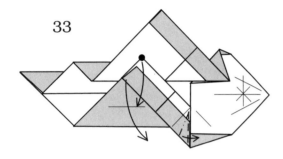

Squash-fold.

34

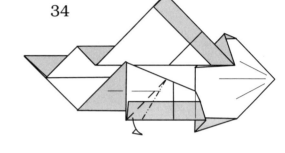

Squash-fold.

35

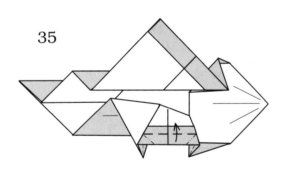

Petal-fold.

36

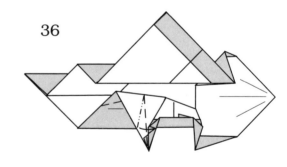

Squash-fold.

37

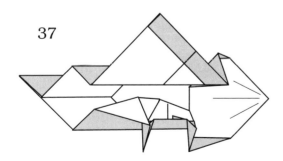

Repeat steps 31–36 on the top.

38

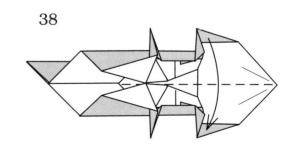

39

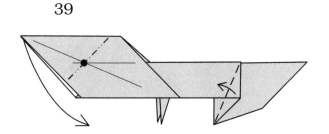

Reverse-fold at the head. Repeat behind at the back legs.

40

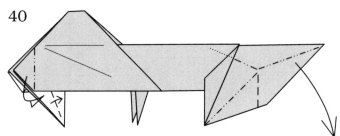

Fold inside and repeat behind at the head. Double-rabbit-ear the tail.

41

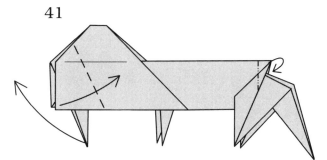

Fold the head at the angle indicated by the next step. Repeat behind. Reverse-fold at the back.

42

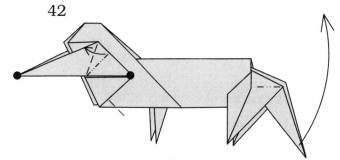

Note that the line between the dots is horizontal. Squash-fold at the mane and repeat behind. Reverse-fold the tail.

43

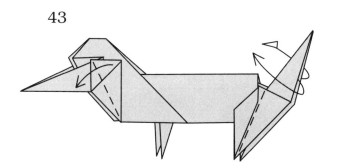

Repeat behind for the mane. Outside-reverse-fold the tail.

44

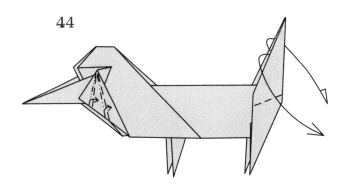

Repeat behind for the mane. Outside-reverse-fold the tail.

Lion 99

45

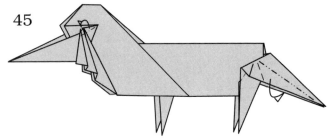

Repeat behind.

46

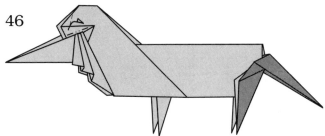

At the hind legs, place the darker paper inside. Repeat behind.

47

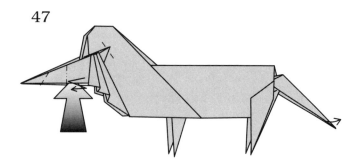

Place your finger underneath the top layer for the reverse folds at the head. Reverse-fold the tip of the ear and repeat behind. Open the tip of the tail.

48

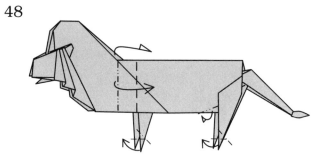

Crimp-fold at the mane. Repeat behind.

49

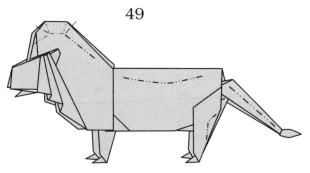

Shape the lion.

50

Lion

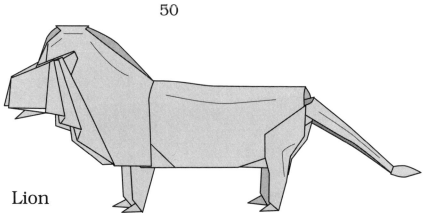

Hippopotamus

I wanted to capture a hippo with head detail, massive body, and short, stubby, rather insignificant legs. It took an interesting folding structure the achieve the right proportions. One corner is hidden by the teeth, two corners are hidden near the front legs, and the last is used for the tail.

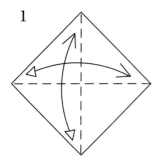

1

Fold and unfold.

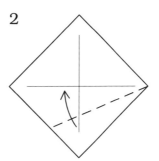

2

Crease lightly.

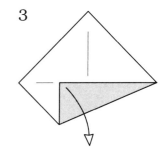

3

Unfold.

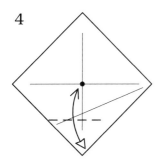

4

Fold up to the center and unfold. Crease lightly and only on the left side.

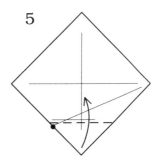

5

Fold up so the dot meets the line above it.

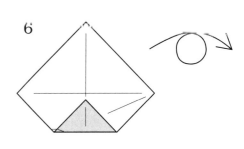

6

7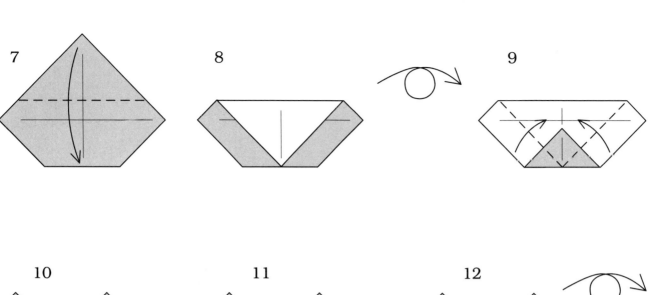

8

9

10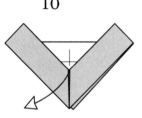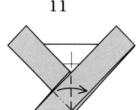

Pull out.

11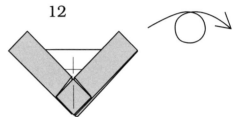

Squash-fold.

12

13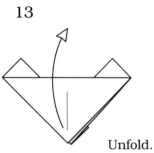

Unfold.

14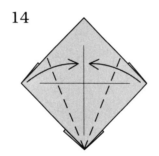

15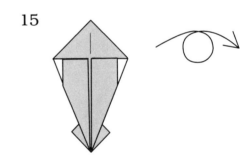

16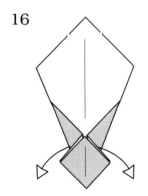

Pull out.

17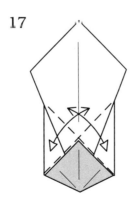

Fold and unfold.

18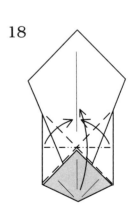

This is similar to the preliminary fold.

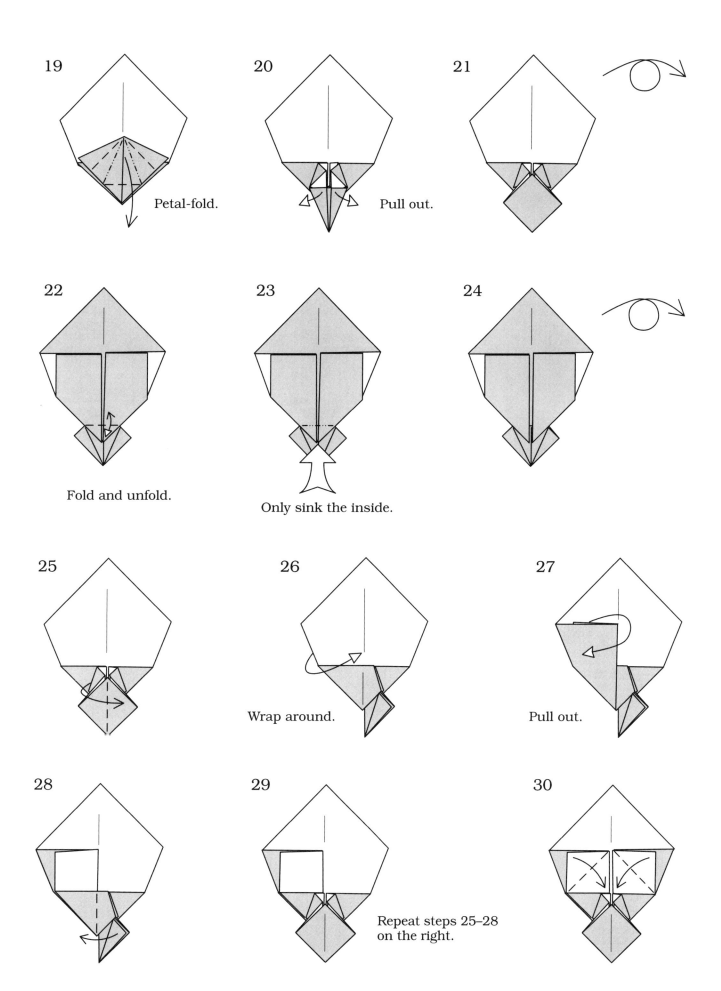

19 Petal-fold.

20 Pull out.

21

22 Fold and unfold.

23 Only sink the inside.

24

25

26 Wrap around.

27 Pull out.

28

29 Repeat steps 25–28 on the right.

30

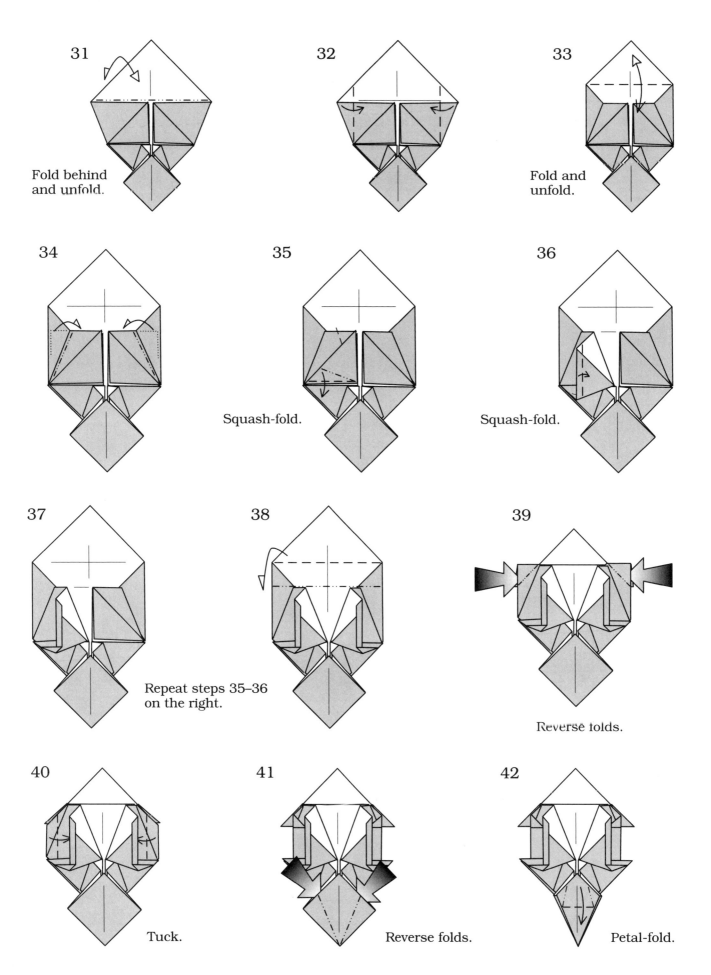

31 Fold behind and unfold.

32

33 Fold and unfold.

34

35 Squash-fold.

36 Squash-fold.

37

38 Repeat steps 35–36 on the right.

39 Reverse folds.

40 Tuck.

41 Reverse folds.

42 Petal-fold.

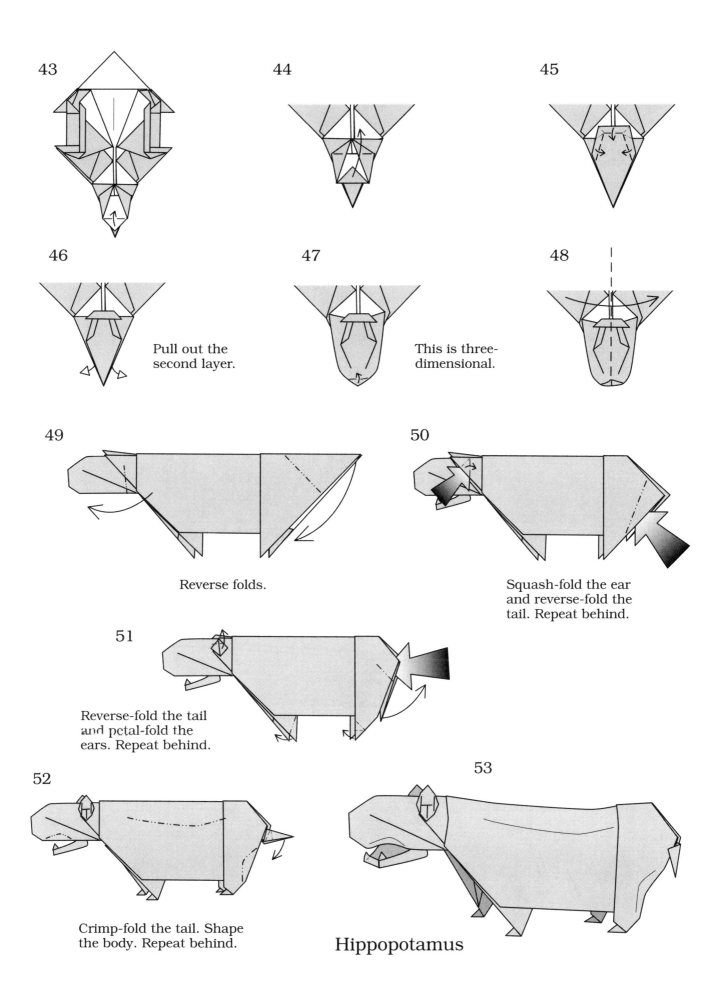

43

44

45

46

Pull out the
second layer.

47

This is three-
dimensional.

48

49

Reverse folds.

50

Squash-fold the ear
and reverse-fold the
tail. Repeat behind.

51

Reverse-fold the tail
and petal-fold the
ears. Repeat behind.

52

Crimp-fold the tail. Shape
the body. Repeat behind.

53

Hippopotamus

Crocodile

Though most of my designs use diagonal fold symmetry, this crocodile uses book fold symmetry. This allows the four corners to be used for the feet with toes. Many crimp folds are used to capture this shape.

1

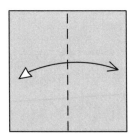

Fold and unfold.

2

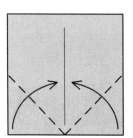

3

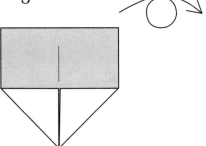

4

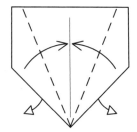

5

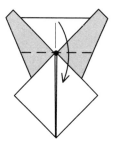

6

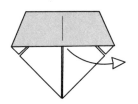

Unfold everything.

7

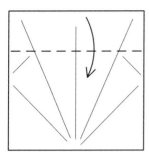

8

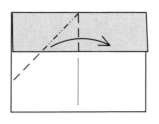

Squash-fold.

9

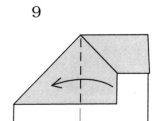

10

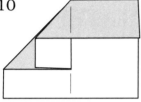

Repeat steps 8–9
on the right.

11

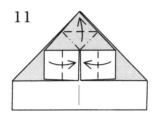

Petal-fold.

12

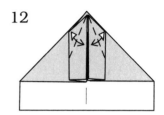

Fold to the center
and unfold.

13

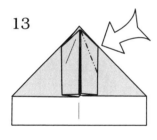

Sink.

14

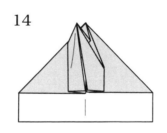

A three-dimensional figure
showing the sink fold.

15

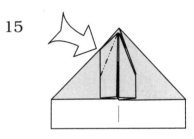

Sink.

16

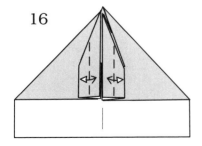

Fold to the center
and unfold.

17

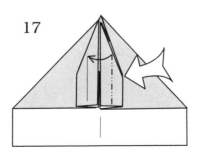

Spread-squash-fold.

18

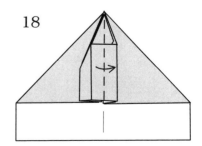

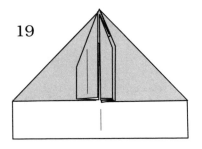

19

Repeat steps 16–18 on the left.

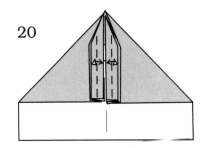

20

Fold and unfold.

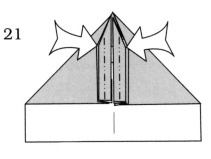

21

Sink.

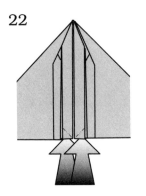

22

Four small reverse folds.

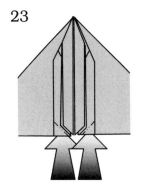

23

Two reverse folds.

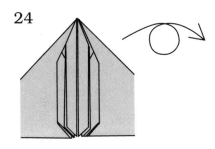

24

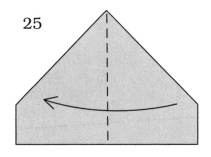

25

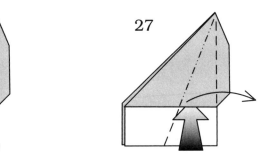

26

Fold and unfold.

27

Squash-fold.

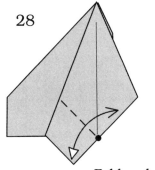

28

Fold and unfold.

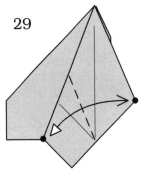

29

Fold and unfold.

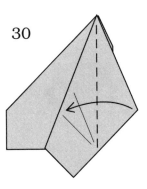

30

31

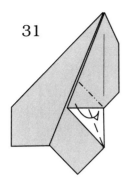

32

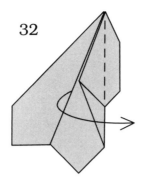

33

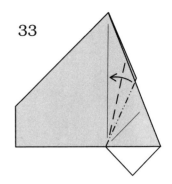

34

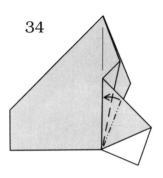

35

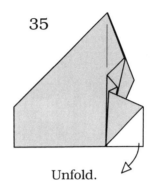

Unfold.

36

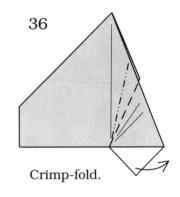

Crimp-fold.

37

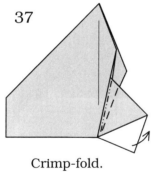

Crimp-fold.

38

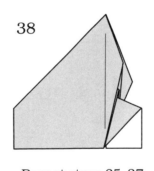

Repeat steps 25–37
on the left.

39

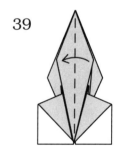

40

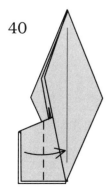

41

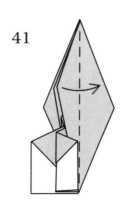

42

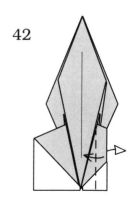

43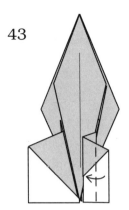

44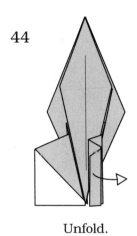

Unfold.

45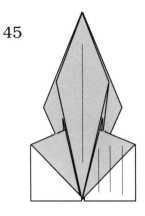

Repeat steps 39–44
on the left.

46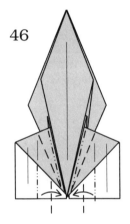

Crimp folds.

47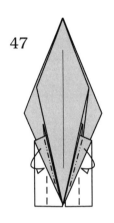

48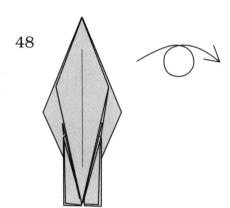

49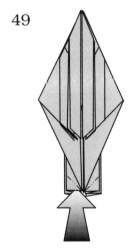

Four reverse folds.

50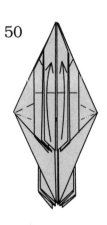

Stretch folds.

51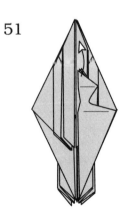

This is a three dimensional
intermediate step on the right
side. Continue stretching and
repeat on the left.

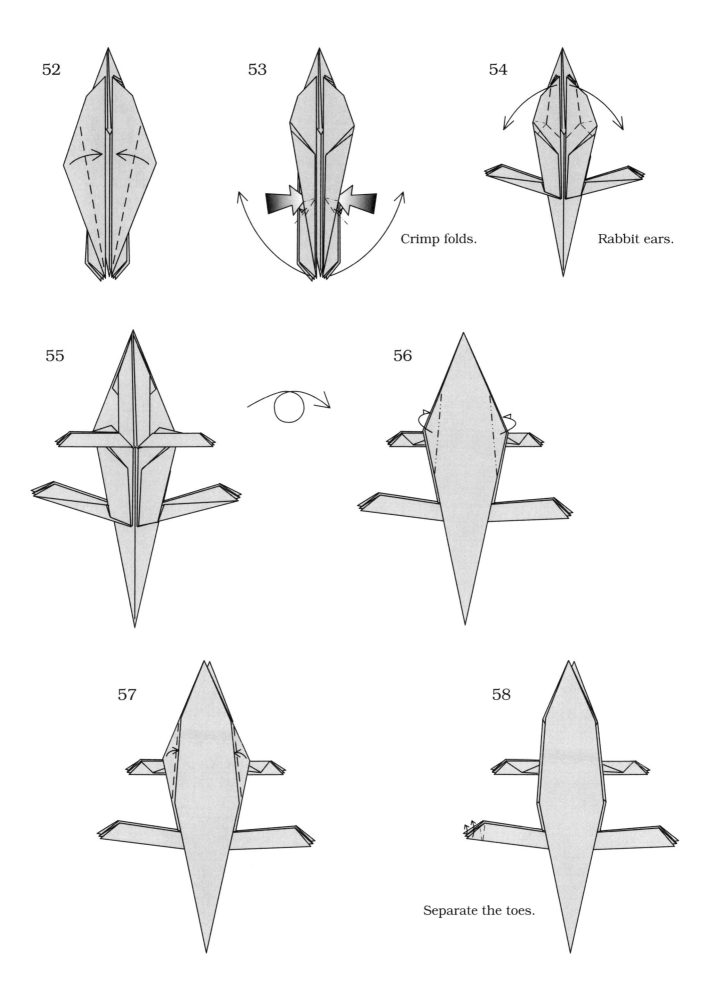

52

53

Crimp folds.

54

Rabbit ears.

55

56

57

58

Separate the toes.

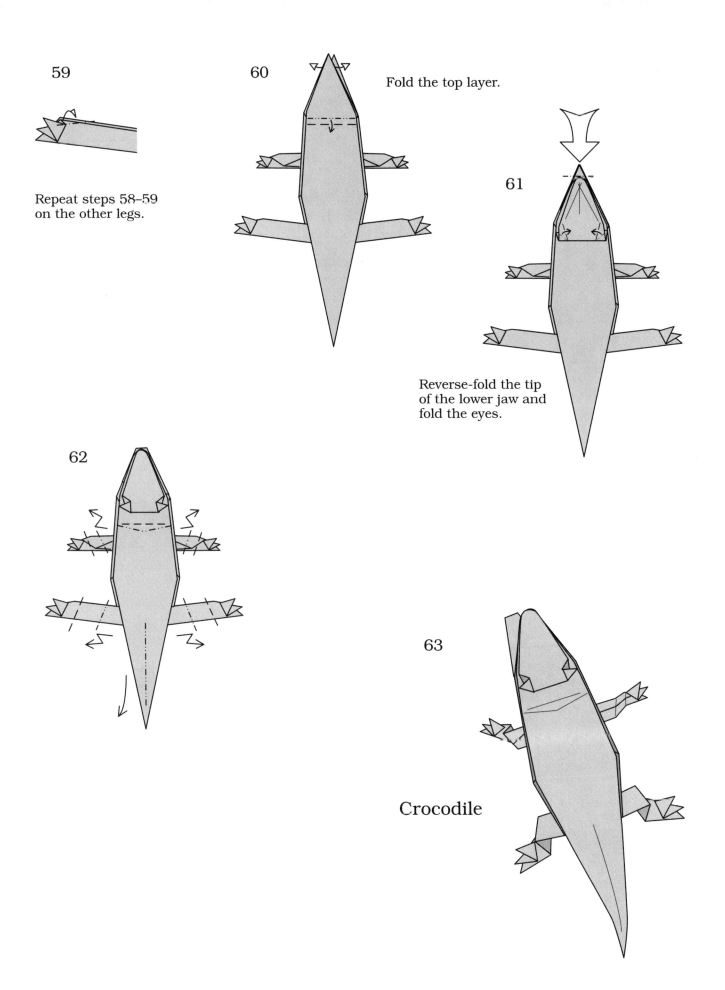

59

Repeat steps 58–59
on the other legs.

60   Fold the top layer.

61   Reverse-fold the tip
of the lower jaw and
fold the eyes.

62

63

Crocodile

Horse with Rider

It is an interesting challenge to create a horse with rider, from just one square. This uses a combination of techniques beginning with a form of the blintz frog base in step 11. Then on one side it has a stretched bird base (step 17), and on the other, there is half of a frog base (step 23). Recall that in a blintz fold, the four corners of the square are folded to the center forming a smaller square, step 3, with added points. Three of the corners are used for the horse—its head and hind legs—while the remaining corner is used for the rider's hat.

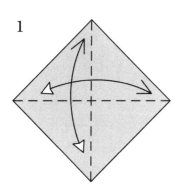

1

Fold and unfold.

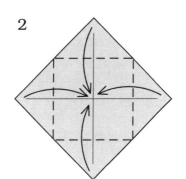

2

Blintz-fold.

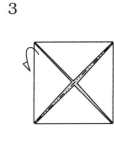

3

Fold behind and rotate.

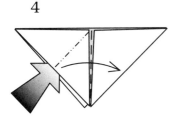

4

Squash-fold.

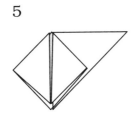

5

Repeat step 4 behind.

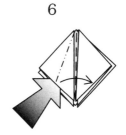

6

Squash-fold.

7

Petal-fold.

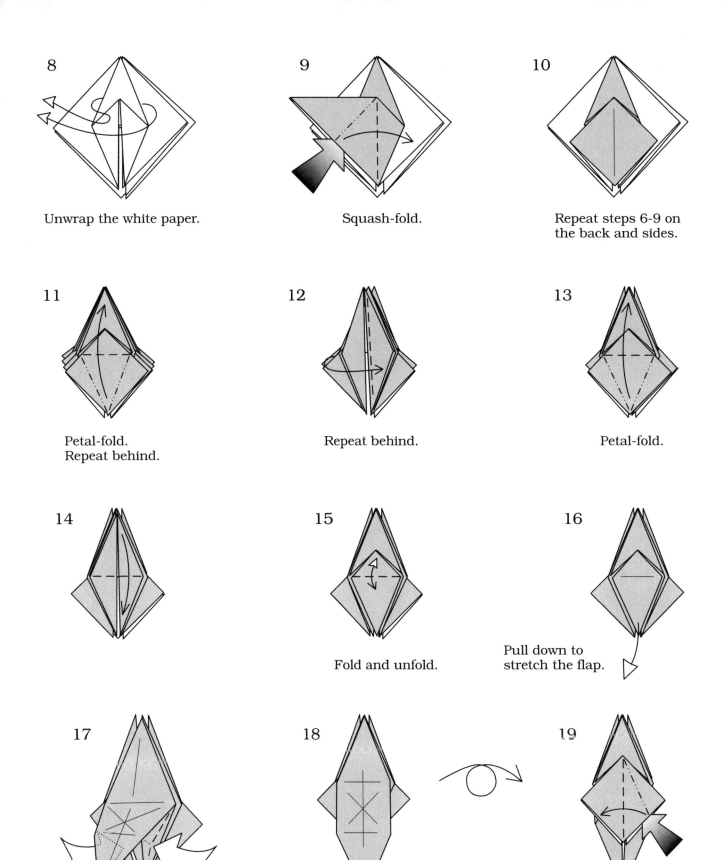

8

Unwrap the white paper.

9

Squash-fold.

10

Repeat steps 6-9 on the back and sides.

11

Petal-fold.
Repeat behind.

12

Repeat behind.

13

Petal-fold.

14

15

Fold and unfold.

16

Pull down to stretch the flap.

17

This is a three-dimensional drawing. Continue stretching.

18

19

Squash-fold.

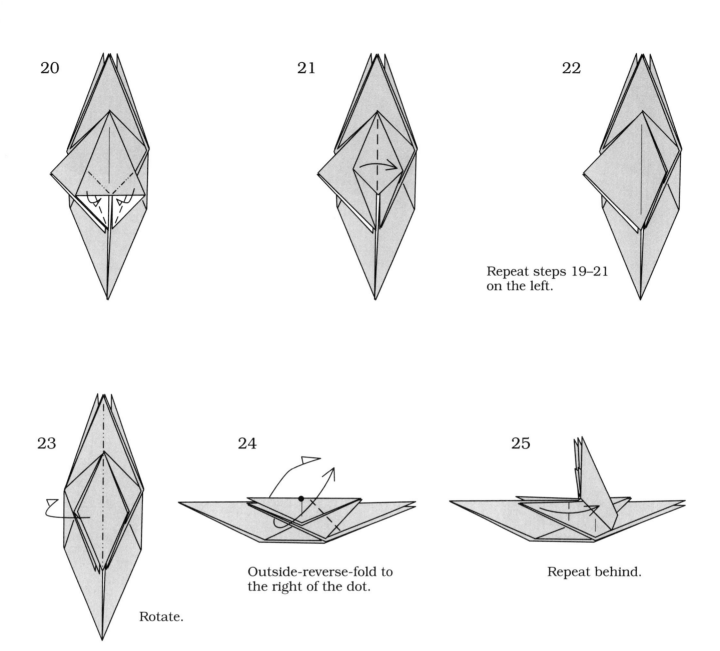

20

21

22

Repeat steps 19–21
on the left.

23

Rotate.

24

Outside-reverse-fold to
the right of the dot.

25

Repeat behind.

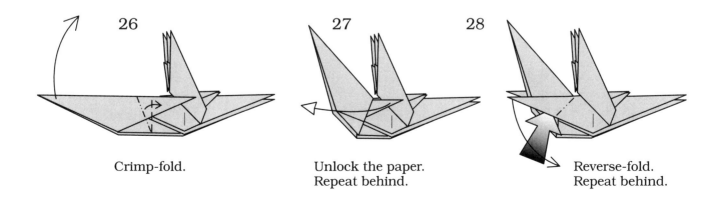

26

Crimp-fold.

27

Unlock the paper.
Repeat behind.

28

Reverse-fold.
Repeat behind.

29

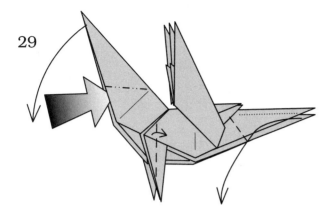

Reverse-fold the head. Valley-fold
the hind leg and also the upper
layer of the front leg. Repeat behind.

30

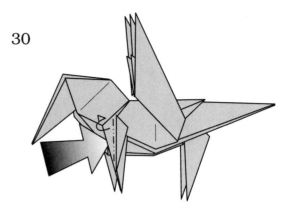

Repeat behind.

31

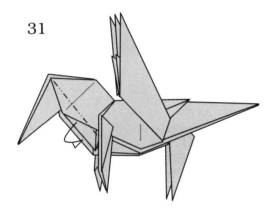

Repeat behind.

32

Outside-reverse-fold the
head. Double-rabbit-ear
the leg and repeat behind.

33

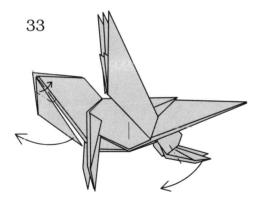

Crimp-fold the head.
Reverse-fold the leg
and repeat behind.

34

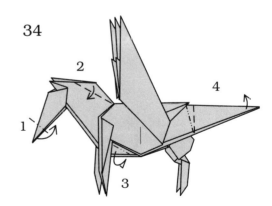

1. Reverse-fold.
2. Fold down on one side.
3. Repeat behind.
4. Crimp-fold.

35

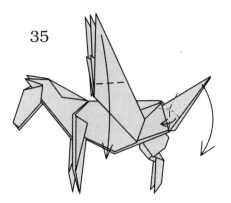

Repeat behind.

36

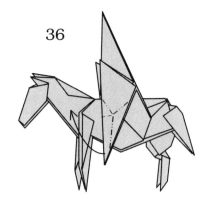

Double-rabbit-ear.
Repeat behind.

37

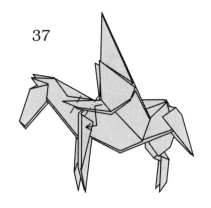

Reverse folds.
Repeat behind.

38

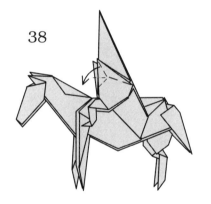

Rabbit-ear.
Repeat behind.

39

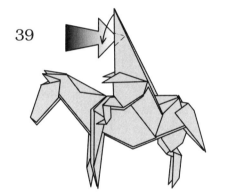

Open the hat.

40

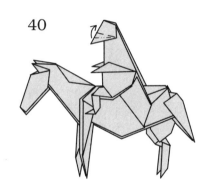

Crimp-fold.

41

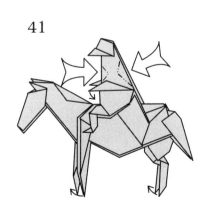

Repeat behind.

42

Horse with Rider

Basic Folds

Rabbit Ear.

To fold a rabbit ear, one corner is folded in half and laid down to a side.

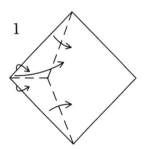

Fold a rabbit ear.

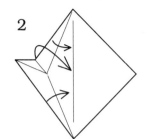

A three-dimensional intermediate step.

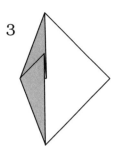

Double Rabbit Ear.

If you were to bend a straw you would be folding the double rabbit ear.

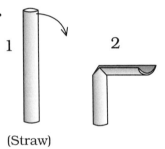

(Straw)

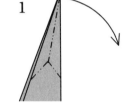

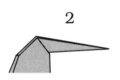

Make a double rabbit ear.

Squash Fold.

In a squash fold, some paper is opened and then made flat. The shaded arrow shows where to place your finger.

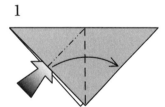

Squash-fold.

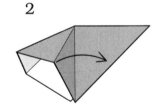

A three-dimensional intermediate step.

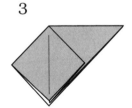

Petal Fold.

In a petal fold, one point is folded up while two opposite sides meet each other.

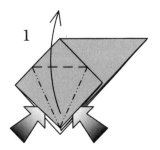

Petal-fold.

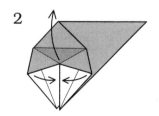

A three-dimensional intermediate step.

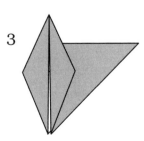

Inside Reverse Fold.

In an inside reverse fold, some paper is folded between layers. Here are two examples.

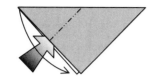

Reverse-fold.

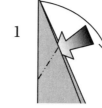

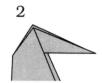

Reverse-fold.

Outside Reverse Fold.

Much of the paper must be unfolded to make an outside reverse fold.

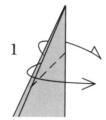

Outside-reverse-fold.

Crimp Fold.

A crimp fold is a combination of two reverse folds.

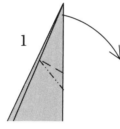

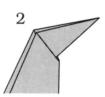

Crimp-fold.

Sink Fold.

In a sink fold, some of the paper without edges is folded inside. To do this fold, much of the model must be unfolded.

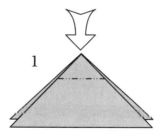

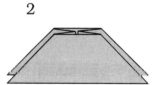

Sink.

Spread Squash Fold.

A cross between a squash fold and sink fold, some paper in the center is spread apart and then made flat.

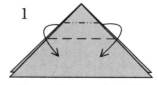

Spread-squash-fold.

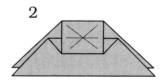